Business Law 1000 Answers to Legal Questions

Authored by

Louis Rubin

Advisory 1

PERSONAL PROPERTY

There are two classes of property, real and personal, and that which distinguishes one from the other is mobility. Land, houses, trees and farms are fixed and immovable and are called real property. A watch, a suit, a piano and an automobile, on the other hand, are movable objects readily transferred from one place to another. Such articles are called personal property.

Sometimes, as in the case of store or house fixtures, there is confusion as to whether an oil burner, for example, is real or personal property. If considered the former, it may not be removed from the premises by a tenant, even if he had it installed himself. If personal property, the tenant may take the oil burner with him—assuming, of course, that it was his.

An article, moreover, may be real property at one time and personal property at another time. A tree standing in its native soil is real property, but if you cut the tree down, and make a pile of wood or use the wood to make a table, it becomes personal property. Oil in the earth. is real property, but if you extract it, you then have an article of merchandise, and the oil becomes personal property. Personal property, too, may be transmuted into real property. Stones, bricks and mortar are all personal property but build a house with them and you have real estate.

Since practically everything people own is classed as personal property, the importance of this subject is obvious. In the main, this branch of the law deals with the bathing question: Who is the legal owner of a disputed piece of property?

Though the bulk of the present chapter is naturally concerned with resolving conflicting claims to such property, patents, trademarks and copyrights are also given the attention they deserve.

Question   You find a wallet containing money, but no writing which identities the owner. Legally, must you advertise for the owner before you can consider the wallet yours?

Answer   No. The obligation is on the part of the loser to advertise for the finder of such property.

Question   While shopping in a grocery store, you notice a five-dollar bill lying on the floor. As you pick up the money, the storekeeper strolls over and asks you for the bill, on the ground, that you found it in his store. May you keep the money or must you turn it over to him?

Answer   You may retain it, providing the real owner is not in the store to claim it. The law takes the view that the money has been lost, not mislaid, and that you have a better claim to it than anyone except the person who lost it. Should the owner later return to ask about the money, the grocer would not be responsible. However, if he has your name and address, he may refer the owner to you.

Question   While riding in a street car, you notice a purse on one of the seats. You pick it up, and, as you are about to step off, the operator of the vehicle, having seen you take the purse, requests that you turn it over to him for safe-keeping. Must you do so?

Answer   Yes. Where property is mislaid on a chair or counter in a store, hotel or street car, the one in possession of the premises, in this case the street car operator, is the proper custodian of the mislaid article, not the one who discovers it.

Question   While walking through the woods with some friends, you stumble over a cardboard box. You and your friends take turns in kicking the box around until it bursts open and $200 in bills come tumbling out. You claim possession of the entire $200. Your friends also claim a share. Who is entitled to it?

Answer   Legally, all of you are entitled to an equal share, in spite of the fact that you were the first one to notice the box. Had you opened the box yourself after stumbling over it, the money would have been yours

Question   Jim finds a wallet in the street. The wallet contains $15 in bills, together with a business card identifying the owner. Must Jim return the wallet?

Answer   Yes. In some states the fact that Jim does not return the wallet, where means of identification are known, may make him guilty of the crime of larceny.

Question   Jim finds a wallet containing $100 in bills, together with a card bearing the owner's name and address. Hurrying to the address stated on the card, Jim informs the owner that, for a reward of

$25, he will be glad to turn the wallet over to him. The owner refuses to offer any reward at all and threatens to call the police if Jim does not instantly deliver the wallet to him. What should Jim do?

Answer Jim should return the wallet to its owner. Indeed, if Jim refuses, the owner may properly have him arrested.

Question A newspaper advertises the following: "Liberal reward will be paid to finder of diamond ring bearing the initials G. T. B. Address Box 124." Having found a ring answering this description, you hasten to the owner's address (which you have learned) and offer to return the ring for the promised reward. The owner offers you $10, an amount which you do not consider liberal enough for the size of the diamond You refuse to return the ring unless you are given a reward of $50. What are your rights in the matter?

Answer None whatever. The offer of a "liberal reward" is often designed to cover up the fact that little or no reward will be given. Legally, the reward advertised must be a definite and specific sum before you can have a lien against it. Where a definite amount is not mentioned in the "ad," the person re, turning the lost article has no comeback.

Question Jim buys a safe and sends it to a mechanic for repairs. The mechanic finds money in the safe. Who is entitled to the money, Jim or the mechanic?

Answer The mechanic, on the theory that the money was lost and that the finder, in this case the mechanic, has a better right to it than anyone else.

Question Tom's sailboat, which was sunk a year ago, is raised from the sea by George who finds $200 in a tin can hidden in the boat. Both boys claim the money. Who is entitled to it?

Answer George, on the legal theory that Tom had abandoned it.

Question Jim finds a pocketbook lying on the counter of a bank, but a bank teller claims it. Who is entitled to the pocketbook?

Answer The teller, on the theory that the pocketbook has not been lost but merely mislaid, thus giving the bank the right to hold it until claimed by the actual owner.

Question Before checking his coat in a night club, Bill puts his gloves in the pocket. Later, the coat is returned to him but not the gloves. Is the owner of the check room responsible?

Answer No, since the gloves were concealed in the coat. The theory is that the check room attendant did not see the gloves being placed in the pocket of the coat; therefore, he would be responsible only for the safekeeping of the coat. Had the attendant seen the gloves placed in the coat, the check room owner would then be responsible for the gloves as well.

Question   You park your automobile in Jackson's parking lot, paying thirty-five cents for the privilege, and receive a ticket which states that the ticket must be surrendered before the car can be taken away. At the request of the parking lot attendant, you leave the ignition key in the car. Later, when you return for the car, you rind that it has been stolen. Is Jackson, the owner of the parking lot, liable?

Answer   Probably. There are two theories of liability. One is that you merely rented parking space, in which case Jackson would not be liable for the theft of the automobile. The other theory is that the transaction amounted to a "bailment," in which case Jackson would be under a duty to exercise reasonable care. His failure to return the car would establish a "prima facie" (at first blush) case of liability on Jackson's part. In the present example, the fact that the key was left in the car lock, so that control of the car was surrendered to Jackson, would be strong evidence to hold Jackson liable.

Question   Henry goes into a restaurant for lunch. He hangs his hat and coat on a hook. When he finishes his meal, the coat is missing. May Henry recover the value of the coat from the restaurant owner?

Answer   No. The coat had not been placed under the care of the restaurant owner or a waiter. A waiter is not expected to guard unchecked coats and hats hung on hooks about the room.

Question   You deposit a suitcase in the parcel room of a railroad station, receiving a check upon which is printed a notice that the railroad's liability for loss is limited to $25. When you call for the suitcase, you are told that it is missing. Actually, the contents and case are worth $250. You have never read the printed notice. May you recover the value and contents of the case instead of $25?

Answer   Yes. Failure of the station master to return your luggage charges him with negligence. It is true that parties to a contract may generally limit liability. But without your actual assent, such agreement is not binding. The fact that you failed to read the printed notice indicates that you never gave your approval to such agreement and hence will not be bound by it.

Question   Mary, before trying on a new coat, lays her own coat on a chair in the presence of the clerk. The coat is stolen. Is the store liable?

Answer   Yes, because the clerk witnessed the placing of Mary's coat on the chair and therefore assumed responsibility for it.

Question   Jim's garage has a sign posted on the wall which says: "Not Responsible for Damage to Automobiles Entrusted to Our Care." Jim has never read the sign. May he recover against the garage owner

	for damage done to his automobile by one of the help?
Answer	Yes. Unless Jim has actually read the notice, he is not bound by it. The question of whether he did or did not actually read the sign then becomes a question of fact to be determined by a jury, or by the court sitting as a jury.
Question	Jim registers in a New York hotel, taking to his room several valuable diamond rings and watches. The hotel has posted notices stating that it has provided a safe for the deposit of valuables. Is the hotel responsible if the jewelry is stolen from Jim's room?
Answer	No. In New York and other states where such notices are posted, the failure of the guest to deposit valuables in the designated safe relieves the hotel of liability. Here, the question is one of statute law. Jim may not plead ignorance, since ignorance of the law is no excuse.
Question	A railroad posts a notice stating that it will not be liable as an insurer for more than $1,000. Jim reads the notice and ships goods worth $5,000. The goods are destroyed in transit. Is the railroad responsible for more than $1,000?
Answer	Yes. A railroad may not limit its liability by posting a general notice, even though the shipper reads it.
Question	Jim delivers a cargo of dairy products for shipment over the railroad. The goods are spoiled in transit because no ice has been provided for their preservation. Is the railroad responsible for the loss?
Answer	Yes. A railroad must exercise the reasonable care consistent with the nature of the goods it undertakes to handle.
Question	Jim delivers fruit to the railroad for shipment to Harry in New Haven. The fruit is transported to New Haven and placed in a warehouse. Before Harry calls for the fruit it is destroyed by rain which comes through a defective roof in the warehouse. Is the railroad responsible?
Answer	Yes. A railroad must keep the goods in a safe place.
Question	Harry goes to a hotel, hands his luggage to a porter, then goes to eat lunch in the grill. His luggage is misplaced and cannot be found. Is the hotel liable?
Answer	Yes. Harry is a guest, in spite of the fact that he did not sign the hotel register. When the porter took charge of his luggage, Harry became a guest of the hotel—at which point liability on the part of the hotel begins.
Question	You spend a week in a hotel, then find you lack sufficient funds to pay your bill. May the hotel retain your luggage as security for the hotel bill?

Answer	Yes. Upon payment of the bill, the luggage must be released. After providing proper notice, the hotel may even sell the luggage in order to secure payment of the bill.
Question	George delivers a coat to his tailor for repairs. When the work is completed, George refuses to pay the bill on the ground that the charge is exorbitant. May the tailor sell the coat to obtain his charges?
Answer	No. The tailor has only the right to retain possession of the coat until he is paid or some agreement is reached.
Question	Jack is called to Harry's house to repair the latter's piano. Harry refuses to pay Jack for his services, claiming the bill is exorbitant. Does Jack have a claim on the piano?
Answer	No. As the piano was always in Harry's custody, Jack lacks the possession required for such claim. He can, however, sue Harry for services rendered.
Question	You take your suit to a cleaner. You later lose your receipt for this suit, and it is found by a stranger who presents it to the cleaner and obtains the suit. May you recover the value of the suit from the cleaner?
Answer	Yes. The cleaner is under a strict obligation to make certain that the right suit is turned over to the right owner.
Question	You deliver an overcoat to a cleaner who agrees to clean, repair and deliver the garment to you by Tuesday of the following week. The garment is not delivered on time, Do you have a claim against the cleaner?
Answer	Yes. The failure to deliver on time constitutes a breach of contract. The question then resolves itself to one of credibility—that is, whether the cleaner is to be believed or the person delivering the overcoat. The burden of proof, as in all damage suits, is on the plaintiff, the party suing, to make out a case. Naturally, the plaintiff makes out a stronger case if he can corroborate his story by means of a witness, where there is no written evidence to support his claim.
Question	A tailor takes in a suit for cleaning, to be delivered when finished. He sends his employee to deliver the suit and the latter disappears, taking the suit with him. The customer demands a new suit. Does he have a claim?
Answer	Yes, on the theory that a breach of contract has been committed.
Question	Bill, accompanied by a friend, leaves some laundry in a drop box outside a laundry establishment. The bundle contains shirts, hose, handkerchiefs and collars. When Bill comes to call for the finished

work, he is told that the laundry never received it. May Bill collect the value of his laundry?

Answer   Yes. If Bill testifies that he dropped the bundle in the drop box and his testimony is corroborated by his friend, he has established a strong case which will be difficult to defeat. The fact that the box is there is an implied invitation to drop bundles in it, and the laundry assumes responsibility. If Bill had no witness, his case would be that much weaker.

Question   Your laundry leaves your bundle outside your apartment door. The bundle is stolen. Is the laundry responsible?

Answer   Yes, Unless you have given instructions for the bundle to be left outside. In that event, you assume the risk; otherwise, the laundry does.

Question   A customer leaves some bundles at his laundry. Later, the establishment is broken into and the laundry stolen. Is the laundry owner liable?

Answer   No, not unless you can prove that the theft was due to the laundry's negligence. Showing that the laundry carelessly left the door open at night might suffice.

Question   A fire breaks out in the laundry, destroying all the garments, including your own. Is the laundry responsible?

Answer   Not unless you can prove that the fire was caused by the laundry owner's negligence. A laundry is not an insurer against theft or loss by fire.

Question   Henry rents a safe deposit box in a bank, placing five War Bonds therein. The bank gives Henry one key, retaining the master key itself, both being necessary to open the box. Burglars enter the vault, break open Henry's safe deposit box, and take his Bonds. Can Henry recover the value of the Bonds from the bank?

Answer   No. If the bank exercises reasonable care, it is not liable; it does not guarantee loss of property against theft.

Question   A friend of yours, a watchmaker, undertakes to repair your watch free of charge. He does it so carelessly, however, that it is damaged. Is he liable?

Answer   Yes, irrespective of whether he was to be paid or not.

Question   Mary borrows Jane's automobile. While the car is in Mary's garage, it is struck by lightning and is totally destroyed. Is Mary liable?

Answer   No. While Mary owes the highest degree of care towards the automobile, she is not liable for loss not caused by her negligence.

Question   Jim erects a ten-story brick building upon his land. He sells the land to Dick. Jim claims title to the building. Is he right?

Answer   No. A sale of the land passes title to Dick, not only to the land, but also to the building on it.

Question A tenant installs a new electric light fixture in his apartment. Upon the termination of the lease, he desires to take the fixture with him. The landlord protests, on the ground that the removal of the fixture will ruin the wall paper. Who is entitled to the fixture?

Answer The tenant. The general rule is that unless the fixture is so firmly attached as to be incapable of removal without great injury to itself or the landlord's property, it may be removed by the tenant. Hangings, tapestry, window blinds and curtains, stoves, cupboards, sheds, grates, steam radiators and their valves and electric refrigerators may be removed by the tenant—assuming, of course, that they are his own.

Question Jim promises Alice a ring for her birthday. Jim buys the ring in Alice's presence; but later, he gives the ring to someone else. Does Alice have a legal claim to the ring?

Answer No. Until the ring is actually delivered to Alice, Jim has a perfect right to change his mind as often as he pleases.

Question Bill writes a number of letters to his wife, saying that he is giving her certain furniture, at the time stored in a warehouse. Bill later changes his mind, refusing to turn over the furniture to his wife. May he be compelled to carry out his promise?

Answer No. There was no gift because there was no delivery. Had he delivered the furniture, there would have been a valid gift and Bill would not later have been able to secure the furniture.

Question Having had a heart attack and expecting to die, Tom gives George his automobile. Tom recovers, goes about his business, and dies eight months later. Tom's estate now claims the automobile. Does George have to give it up?

Answer Yes. Tom's recovery automatically revokes the gift; Tom's estate may rightfully claim the car. Had Tom died within a few days after giving the automobile to George, it would have been a valid gift and George could then have kept it.

Question John has money and bonds in a metal box. He delivers the box to Paul, telling him that he is about to go to the hospital for a serious operation and that, if he should die, Paul is to keep the box. John's operation is successful. Shortly thereafter, however, he dies suddenly of a disease other than that for which the operation was performed. May Paul retain the box?

Answer Yes. Johns gift is called "causa mortis," or on account of death, and is completed with John's delivery of the box and contents. In such gifts it is not necessary that John, the donor, die of the disease from which he apprehended death. A gift of this sort is recognized where death is anticipated from an impending disease or peril. The theory is that it enables the donor to dispose of personal property under circumstances which make the writing of a will impracticable, yet enables the donor to regain title of the thing or article disposed of in the event he recovers.

Question   Tom is engaged to Alice. In anticipation of the marriage he gives her jewelry, furs and a diamond engagement ring. Alice breaks the engagement and marries another man. May Tom get back his gifts?

Answer   Yes. Such gifts are legally said to have been made upon condition that the marriage takes place. Should the marriage not take place, Tom may recover the presents.

Question   James gives Dorothy a wrist watch for a Christmas present. Later, after a quarrel, James demands the return of the watch. Must Dorothy give it up?

Answer   No. Such a gift is made merely to secure the lady's favor and is an unconditional gift.

Question   You sign a pledge to give a church or charity a fifty-dollar contribution. May this promise be legally enforced?

Answer   No, not unless the church or charity incurred obligation the strength of your promised contribution. If it did, your promise can be legally enforced.

Question   You want to change your name from John Slovensky to John Smith. May you do so without going into court?

Answer   Yes. You may change your name as often as you like, so long as there is no intention to defraud.

Question   What objects may be patented?

Answer   The Federal Law provides that "any person who has invented or discovered any new and useful art, machine, manufacture, or composition of matter, or any new and useful improvement thereof, not known or used by others in this country and not patented or described in any printed publication in this or any other foreign country, before his invention or discovery thereof, and not in public use or on sale for more than two years prior to his application, unless the same is proved to have been abandoned, may, upon payment of the fees required by the law, and other due proceedings had, obtain a patent therefor."

Question   In an invention or discovery, what two things are essential before a patent will be granted?

Answer   It must have novelty and utility or usefulness.

Question   How do you go about obtaining a patent?

Answer   The inventor or discoverer must make written application to the Commissioner of Patents in Washington, D. C., and file what is known as a "specification," or written description of the invention or discovery, "and of the manner and process of making, constructing, compounding, and using it, in such full, clear, concise, and exact terms as to enable any person skilled in the art or Science to which it appertains, or with which it is most nearly connected, to make, construct, compound, and use the same. " It is further provided that "in case of a machine he shall explain the principle thereof, and the best mode in which he has contemplated applying that principle, so as to distinguish it from other inventions, and shall particularly point out and distinctly claim the part, improvement, or combination which he claims as his invention or discovery."

Question   What is the next step after this?

Answer   This "specification" and claim must be signed by the inventor and witnessed by two persons. The applicant must also furnish a drawing, specimen or model to illustrate his claim; finally, he must make oath that he believes himself to be the original and first inventor or discoverer of the art, machine, manufacture, composition or improvement for which he seeks a patent; that he does not know and does not believe that the same was ever before known or used; he must also state of what country he is a citizen. All this information, together with the necessary fees, is filed with the Patent Office in Washington, usually through an attorney. A patent is then granted if it appears that the claimant is entitled to one.

Question   Who issues patents?

Answer   They are issued in the name of the United States of America, under the seal of the Patent Office, signed by the Secretary of the Interior and countersigned by the Commissioner of Patents.

Question   For how long a period are patents issued?

Answer   Patents are granted for the term of seventeen years to the patentee, i.e., the person who applies for the patent, giving him the exclusive right to make, use and sell the invention or discovery throughout the United States, and its territories.

Question   Suppose the inventor dies before the patent is issued but after application is made?

Answer   The right to apply for and obtain the patent passes on the heirs of the patentee.

Question   May a patent be assigned or transferred by the inventor to a third party?

Answer   Yes. Not only the patent, but any legal interest in it may be assigned or transferred to a third person, provided the assignment is made in writing. As a precaution and protection, such assignment should be recorded in the Patent Office within three months from its date.

Question   What should an inventor do who wants time to perfect or complete an invention, but who has not yet obtained a patent?

Answer   He should file a "caveat" with the Patent Office, setting forth the design of the invention, and requesting protection of his right until he shall have matured his invention. This caveat is then filed in the confidential archives of the Patent Office. Its effect is to protect the inventor, for one year, against applications which might, in the meantime, be presented by other persons.

Question   What happens when two persons file an application for a patent for the same invention, and both inventions are pending in the Patent Office at the same time?

Answer   The Commissioner of Patents may compel the two interested persons to appear before him and offer evidence as to who was really the first inventor.

Question   What is meant by copyright?

Answer   Copyright is the sole right granted the applicant to print, publish, or sell one's literary, musical, or artistic compositions. The law provides that the application for copyright shall specify to which of the following classes the work belongs: (a) books, including composite or other cyclopedic works, directories, gazetteers, and other compilations; (b) periodicals, including newspapers; (c) lectures, sermons, ad. dresses prepared for oral delivery; (d) dramatic or dramatic musical compositions; (e) musical compositions; (f) maps; (g) works of art; (h) reproductions of works of art; (i) drawings of plastic works of a scientific or technical character; (j) photographs; (k) prints and pictorial illustrations; (l) motion picture plays; (m) motion pictures other than motion picture plays.

Question   How do you go about securing a copyright?

Answer   First, print the work with the copyright notice printed on it—for example, "Copyright, 1945 by John Smith"; or, in the case of works specified above, (f) to (k), the notice may consist of the letter C enclosed in a circle, thus ©, accompanied by the initials, monogram or symbol of the owner—provided his name appears on some accessible part of the copies.
           Second, send to the Register of Copyrights, Library of Congress, Washington, D. C., two copies of the work, together with an application for registration. The copies deposited must be accompanied by an affidavit, stating that the typesetting, printing and binding of the book, etc. have been performed within the United States.

Question   Where do you secure such affidavit forms and application blanks?

Answer   From the Copyright Office, Library of Congress, Washington, D. C.

Question For what period of time does a copyright protect the author or owner?

Answer Twenty-eight years. However, within one year prior to the expiration of the twenty-eight years, the owner, or his next of kin, may secure a renewal for another twenty-eight years.

Question What is the fee for a copyright?

Answer Four dollars. This includes the certificate from the Registor of Copyrights under seal.

Question May a copyright be assigned to another?

Answer Yes, provided the assignment is in writing.

Question What is a trademark?

Answer A trademark is a distinctive word, emblem, symbol or device, or a combination of these, used on goods actually sold in commerce to indicate or identify the manufacturer or seller of the goods.

Question Where are trademarks registered?

Answer With the Commissioner of Patents, Patent Office, Washington, D. C.

Question How do you get a trademark registered?

Answer Under the law, the Commissioner of Patents is required to establish classes of merchandise for the purpose of trademark regulation and registration. There are forty-nine different classes. One application for the registration of a trademark will cover only goods belonging to one class. If the applicant desires to register his goods for trademark under any other class, he is required to file another application. The fee is $10 with each application. The application must consist of a drawing of the trademark to be registered, made in India ink on sheets of Bristol board of a particular size and shape. Five specimens or facsimiles of the mark must be filed with the application, together with the applicant's affidavit. After the registration is filed it is examined, and if it appears to the examiner to be a mark that can properly be registered, the Commissioner of Patents gives public notice in the Official Gazette for Registration that such a mark has been applied for.

Question For how long a period is a trademark registered?

Answer Twenty years; and it may be renewed.

Advisory 2

CONTRACTS

The law of contracts is an integral part of the commercial world. Indeed, it is virtually impossible to transact any business without agreements, oral or written.

A verbal. contract is a cultural hang-over from the days when our ancestors could neither read nor write. Today, while such contracts are in many cases perfectly binding, the prudent business man will invariably reduce them to written form. He should do this as a matter of self-interest, so that when disputes arise he may refer directly to the written instrument containing the terms agreed upon in a permanent form. It is bad enough when a question of interpretation comes up. Think how much worse it is when there is not even a writing to refer to!

The chief disadvantage of an oral contract, then, is that it is so difficult to prove. Courts, in such cases, have only the word of one interested person against that of another, and a stalemate is apt to result. To make certain that a verbal agreement is carried out according to the terms originally agreed upon, it is wise to have a witness present at the time the contract is made.

Breaches of contract occur, of course, irrespective of whether they are oral or written. Courts are cluttered with such cases. The plaintiff, the party suing, comes to court demanding damages for the broken contract. With the burden of proof upon him, the plaintiff must show not only that the contract has been breached, but that he has sustained damages as a result. The defendant, the party being sued, on the other hand, comes to court prepared to prove that he lived up faithfully to his agreement, or, if he did in fact break it, that he did so for good and sufficient reasons.

Question   What is a contract?
Answer   A contract is an agreement between two or more persons to do or
           not to do a particular thing.

14

Question   What are the essential elements of a binding contract?

Answer   There must be, first, the consent or agreement of two or more persons expressed by the offer of one of the parties and the acceptance of that offer by another. For example, an offer is made to me by a publisher to write a book. I accept the offer.

Second, there must be a definite object which constitutes the subject matter of the agreement; in this case, the book. Third, the agreement must be based upon a consideration; that is, the price, motive or inducement for the contract. In this case, the consideration would be the amount of money I receive for writing the book.

Fourth, the persons who make the promise must be legally capable of entering into that particular kind of contract. Since the publisher is of legal age and I am over twenty-one, we can enter into such an agreement.

Fifth, the consent of the parties must be real and genuine. The persons making the promise must mean what they say; their consent must not be secured by fear, fraud or error. The publisher, for example, must enter into his part of the

bargain freely, really expecting to publish the book according to the terms of the contract. As the author, I must write the book and deliver it in accordance, with the terms of the written contract. Both of us must enter into the agreement without any fraudulent intent or misrepresentation.

Finally, the subject matter of the agreement must be lawful. The publishing of a book on law is lawful.

Question   What contracts are required to be in writing?

Answer   (1) A special promise by an executor or administrator to pay damages out of his own pocket rather than the estate over which he is administrating. Suppose, for example, you are the administrator of your father's estate. Someone has a claim against your father and is pressing you, as his administrator, for payment. If you want to assume the obligation yourself, you must agree in writing to pay the claim. Otherwise, you are not bound.

(2) Any promise to answer for the debt, default or miscarriage of another. For example, you promise to pay your friend's debt. To make you liable, your promise must be in writing. A verbal promise will not bind you.

(3) Agreements made in consideration of marriage. Thus, a verbal promise made before marriage to make a settlement after marriage is unenforceable. The promise must be in

writing. For example, you are planning to marry Tim who promises to settle $5,000 on you after marriage. For this promise to be binding, Tim must put it in writing.

(4) Contracts for the sale of land or real estate or any interest in them. However, a contract for the erection of a building is considered a contract for work and material, not for an interest in land, and need not—though for practical purposes it always should—be in writing.

(5) Agreement not to be performed before one year from the making thereof. For example, you promise to sell your car to someone a year from now, at a certain price and under certain conditions. To be binding on you, that promise must be in writing.

Question   What should one look for in examining a contract?

Answer   The chief thing is to make certain that the written contract embodies all the terms agreed upon by the parties. Everything that is agreed upon verbally should be included in the written instrument. The contract should be definite and precise, and should contain a clear, intelligent statement of the terms. Beware of vague or ambiguous words or phrases. Finally, and most important, when in doubt as to whether the written agreement correctly and accurately expresses your conception of the contract, don't sign! Instead, consult your lawyer.

Question   For what contracts are infants, i. e., those under twenty one years of age, liable?

Answer   Generally, they are liable for such necessaries as food, shelter, clothing, medical and dental care, and education suitable to their station in life. Only the reasonable value of the necessaries purchased by them can be recovered, not the contract price.

Question   Janet, who is eighteen, contracts to buy an automobile. She pays $200 down and gives notes for the balance. After driving the car for a few weeks, she returns it to the dealer and demands her money back. May she recover it?

Answer   Yes, an automobile is not considered a necessity; being under twenty-one, Janet may avoid the agreement.

Question   Bill, age twenty, buys a motorcycle on the installment plan, after paying part of the purchase price as a down payment. Unable to maintain the installment payments, Bill defaults and the motorcycle is taken from him. What can he do?

Answer   He may recover the down payment, as well as any

installments he may have made. Had he been twenty-one or over, all the money would have been lost and a judgment could be entered for the balance of the installments yet due.

Question   Ed, who falsely represents himself to be twenty-three but who is actually nineteen, purchases an automobile on the installment plan. When he fails to make his payments, the car is seized by the finance company which files suit for the balance of the installments. May the company recover?

Answer   No. Most courts hold that an infant is not liable when he falsely represents himself as being of age. Ed, therefore, may demand all his money back, including the down payment.

Question   Ted, age twenty, buys a wrist watch on the installment plan. After he reaches twenty-one, he wishes to return the watch and get back the money he has paid. Can he do so?

Answer   Yes. He has the privilege of either affirming or disavowing the contract when he reaches his majority.

Question   Is a lunatic liable for his contracts, including necessaries?

Answer   No. The contract may be avoided by the lunatic when he recovers his reason, or by the committee appointed by the court to care for him. However, a contract entered into by a lunatic with a person unaware of his condition will not relieve the lunatic of liability unless he returns the article or merchandise involved.

Question   A drunkard goes into a pawn shop and buys a diamond ring for which he pays $500. Next day, when sober, he seeks to return the ring and get his money Can he legally do so?

Answer   Yes. A contract made by a person so intoxicated at the time as not to know what he is doing may be avoided at his option.

Question   You are sent Christmas seals which you don't use. Are you obliged to pay for them?

Answer   No. Legally you are under no obligation to return them either, for you never accepted the offer.

Question   A tie company sends you a half-dozen ties which you use knowing that the manufacturer expects payment for them. Are you under any obligation to pay for them, assuming that you never ordered them in the first place?

Answer   Yes. The use of the ties constitutes the acceptance of them. However, if you had not used them you would be required to either return or pay for them.

Question   A publisher of a magazine notifies you that your subscription will be renewed unless he is notified to the contrary. You do not answer his letter and he continues to send you the magazine. Are you obliged to pay for the periodical?

Answer   No. Since you did not ask for the renewal, you are neither obliged to pay nor to be put to the trouble or expense of returning the magazines.

Question   Tom writes Henry: "I offer to sell you one hundred sin of stock at fifty dollars per share, and unless I hear from you by next Tuesday I shall conclude that you have accepted my offer." Tom receives no word from Henry. Is there a contract?

Answer   No. Henry is under no obligation to get in touch with Tom.

Question   A bookseller's catalog, with prices stated alongside the titles of the books, is sent through the mails. A dozen requests come in for a first edition of "David Copperfield." May the bookseller refuse to sell the book to any of the twelve individuals?

Answer   Yes. A catalog is an invitation to do business but is not a legal offer to sell.

Question   Jones, a manufacturer, sends a circular letter to a jobber which reads as follows: "We have prepared and are sending under this cover a printed document setting forth the terms and conditions on which Jones Bicycles will be supplied to the wholesale trade. Hereafter, no order will be filled except on the terms set forth in the enclosed document." The job sends in an order for bicycles on the terms stated, but the manufacturer refuses to fill it. May the jobber insist that the order be filled?

Answer   No. Such circulars are not considered offers to sell; they are merely invitations for orders which the manufacturer may fill or not, as he pleases.

Question   Smith offers by letter, dated June 28th, to purchase shares in the Stonewall Hotel Company. No answer is given him until November 15th when he is informed by the company that shares are allotted him. Must be take the shares?

Answer   No. More than a reasonable time has elapsed between the offer and acceptance, and the original offer is considered revoked. What constitutes a reasonable time is usually a question of fact to be determined by a jury.

Question   The Smith Fertilizer Company agrees by letter to sell some fertilizer to Farmer Harrison, at a stipulated price. It is decided by the parties that a written contract should be executed by them, embodying the terms already agreed upon. Shortly afterward, The Smith Fertilizer Company writes Farmer Harrison, enclosing the formal contract with the request that he sign and return it, stating that, upon receipt, The Smith Company will forward a properly executed duplicate. Farmer Harrison signs the contract and returns it to the company which subsequently refuses to sign, or deliver the promised duplicate, and repudiates the agreement. Is the Smith Company compelled to carry out its agreement?

Answer   Yes. It will be bound by the original letter containing the terms of the agreement.

Question   Benson gives a letter to Cummings, addressed to Brown. In effect, the letter states that Cummings wants to purchase $2,500 worth of furniture and that if Brown extends the credit, Benson will guarantee payment of the bill. Cummings presents the letter on July 15th, and Brown sells and delivers the furniture. That same day, Benson discovers that Cummings is heavily in debt and immediately writes to Brown, withdrawing his offer. On July 16th, Brown dictates a letter to Benson advising him of the sale in reliance of the latter's guarantee, but before the letter can be typed, Brown receives Benson's letter of revocation. Brown sends the letter to Benson as dictated. Is Benson liable?

Answer   Yes. The offer of guaranty became binding when Brown extended the requested credit. Since Brown accepted and completed the sale before Benson's letter of revocation was received, the revocation is ineffective.

Question   The X Company, writing from London on October 1st, makes an offer to the Blank Manufacturing Company in New York, asking for a reply by cable. The Blank Company receives the offer on October 10th and at once accepts in the manner requested. On October 8th, however, the X Company mails a letter revoking the offer. Is the X Company bound by the original offer?

Answer   Yes. The fact that the Blank Company accepted the offer, before receiving notice of revocation, makes it a binding agreement. In this case, the offer was accepted on October 10th and the contract went into effect as of that date.

Question   Smith, in Louisville, mails a letter accepting an offer received by mail from Brown in Baltimore. A day before Brown receives the letter, Smith wires Brown that the letter is on its a way, stating that, having changed his mind, he is countermanding his acceptance. Is Smith liable?

Answer   Yes. Since the offer was sent by mail, the acceptance became effective—and a contract created—when the acceptance was mailed.

Question   Without previous negotiations, the Jones Fur Company has several times sent shipments of fur skins to Fisher, who each time, accepted and paid for the skins. The Jones Fur Company again sends Fisher a shipment of skins. This time, Fisher finds them unsatisfactory, lets them lie in his warehouse for several months and takes no steps to notify the Jones Company. While in the warehouse, the skins are destroyed by accidental fire. The Jones Fur Company now sues Fisher for the market price of the skins. Can it recover?

Answer   Yes. Previous dealings between the parties impose a duty on Fisher to promptly notify the seller as to whether or not he is going to keep the skins.

Question   A newspaper advertises a subscription contest, offering to give cash prizes to the winners. The rules governing the contest are stated and the right to amend the rules reserved. Tom, as a contestant, sends in some subscriptions. At the beginning of the last week of the contest, the newspaper publishes a notice that henceforth only certified checks or money orders will be received for subscriptions. Later that same day, Tom, unaware of the change in the rules, sends in some additional subscriptions accompanied by checks which are not certified. The checks are accepted and cashed, but are not credited to Tom in the contest. Tom receives third prize, but he would have won first prize if he had been credited with all his subscriptions. If he sues, can he collect first-prize money?

Answer   Yes. The acceptance and cashing of the checks makes the newspaper liable.

Question   You ask the owner of a house at what price he is willing to sell it. The owner replies by naming a price which you accept. Is this a binding contract?

Answer   No. This is not binding because the price mentioned does not necessarily mean that the owner would sell it to you at that figure.

Question George, the owner of a house, writes a letter to Ralph saying that if Ralph will appear at a certain time and place with the price in cash, he will receive a deed to the property. Ralph appears with the money, but George fails to show up. May Ralph compel George to go through with the deal?

Answer No. When George fails to show up, the offer is revoked.

Question John offers to sell his house to Bill for $3,500. Bill replied by offering $3,000 which is refused. Bill then tells John that he will pay the $3,500 originally asked, but now John refuses
to sell. May Bill compel John to go through with the deal at $3,500?

Answer No. When John's first offer was refused there was no acceptance and hence no contract. Bill's later offer of $3,500 is a new offer altogether which may be accepted or rejected at John's option.

Question Suppose, in the above case, Bill had merely asked John if he would consider taking $3,000 instead of $3,500, without definitely refusing to pay $3,500. Would it be a binding contract?

Answer Yes. A simple inquiry as to whether John would change his terms does not amount to a rejection.

Question Brown writes Smith, offering to sell the former's house for $5,000. Smith writes back, but offers only $4,500. A few hours later, having changed his mind, Smith wires Brown, agreeing to buy the house for $5,000. The wire, of course, reaches Brown before the letter. Brown now refuses to sell the house for $5,000. Can he be compelled to do so?

Answer Yes. An offer is not effective until communicated to the party making it. When Smith wired agreeing to pay $5,000, the wire having reached Brown sooner than the letter, the contract was made. A rejection, like a revocation, does not destroy the original offer until actually communicated.

Question John sends a magazine article to a publisher. Not hearing from him for three or four months, John writes to make inquiry concerning the manuscript. The editor replies that he is very sorry but the manuscript is lost. John does not have a carbon copy. Does he have a claim against the publisher?

Answer	When one sends a manuscript to a publisher the latter is bound to take care of it for a reasonable time, since his business constitutes an asking of offers from the public. The publisher, on the facts mentioned above, would be liable in damages. To avoid liability, the editor must return the manuscript, if rejected, within a reasonable time.
Question	Brown offers to buy Smith's house for $10,000. The offer is accepted. Before anything is done to effect the transfer of the property, however, Brown dies. What are Smith's rights?
Answer	None. The death of the offeror, Brown, prior to the performance of any part of the act called for by the offer, cancels the offer. Hence, Brown's acceptance is ineffective.
Question	Tom enters Henry's employment under a contract whereby the latter agrees to give Tom, in addition to a salary of $50 per week, a "fair share of the profits of the business," to be determined on January 1st. On January 1st Henry refuses to give Tom any share at all. Does Tom have a legal claim against Henry?
Answer	No. The contract is too vague to be enforced. To be binding, the agreement must clearly state what share of the profits Tom is to receive.
Question	Charles agrees to buy five acres of land out of more than ten offered by James, but without specifying which five acres. Charles gives James a $500 deposit, but later demands his money back. May he recover the deposit?
Answer	Yes. If five specific acres had been mentioned, together with their boundaries, the agreement would be binding. As it is, the contract is too vague and uncertain to be enforced.
Question	You rent a grocery store from Henry, requesting him to give you the "first chance" to buy the property in case it should be for sale. No price is named. Henry agrees. Later, Henry sells the property containing the grocery store to someone else. What can you do about it?
Answer	Nothing, since the agreement is vague as to price, terms, etc.
Question	John promises to give his niece a house and provide for her at his death if she will live with him. She does. After John's death, the niece learns that her uncle has not provided for her as promised. Does she have a claim against the estate?
Answer	No. Such agreements are held to be too indefinite and

vague to be enforced.

Question Bill enters into a written agreement with the Blank Drug Company by which the latter employs him as manager of one of its chain drug stores. The contract provides that it shall continue in force until both parties declare their intention to cancel it. Six months after being employed, Bill receives a better offer and leaves his employer. Bill is sued for breach of contract. Will the Blank Drug Company recover?

Answer No. Such agreements are generally held invalid due to uncertainty as to the length of employment; To be effective, the agreement must be specific; it must state, exactly, the period of time covered by the, contract.

Question A reward of $500 is offered for the arrest and conviction of Jones, a murderer. Intending to claim the reward, Tom pursues Jones and kills him while making the arrest. May Tom claim the reward?

Answer Yes. The terms "arrest and conviction" have been complied with when a fugitive is killed during an attempt to arrest him.

Question A reward is offered for the arrest and conviction of a criminal. Through your efforts, the criminal is arrested and placed in jail pending trial; while there the criminal commits suicide. Are you entitled to the reward?

Answer No. The conditions of the reward are not fulfilled. The criminal has been arrested but not convicted.

Question A reward is offered for the detection and arrest of certain criminals who set fire to a building. A policeman arrests Bill who is later convicted as the crime. May the officer claim the reward?

Answer A police officer cannot recover a reward where the services he performs are those within his official duty.

Question Mrs. Smith tells a policeman that if he will arrest Mrs. White, who has just struck her, she will pay the officer $50. Mrs. White is arrested and the policeman demands his money. Is he entitled to it?

Answer No. In making the arrest he has done only what he is legally bound to do. Hence, there is no legal consideration for Mrs. Smith's promise.

Question Alice, Bill's wife, leaves his home without just cause. In, order to induce her to return, Bill gives Alice his note for $1,000. Alice returns and later files suit on the note against Bill. Can she recover?

Answer	No. The obligation to live with Bill is imposed by law and Alice's return is nothing more than the law requires of her. Hence Bill's written promise is without legal consideration.
Question	Tom enters into an agreement to build a house for Ralph. He finds the conditions much more difficult than he had reason to anticipate. Tom tells Ralph that, because of the unforeseen difficulties and the additional expense involved, he will not be able to go through with the contract. In order to induce Tom to go ahead, Ralph promises him an extra $1,000 to complete the contract. Tom does complete the work but Ralph now refuses to pay the additional money. Must he?
Answer	Generally speaking, no. Courts usually hold that Tom is only doing what he should have done in the first place and is not entitled to extra payment.
Question	An uncle promises to give his nephew $1,500 if the latter will stop drinking and smoking until he reaches twenty-one years of age. The boy does stop. A few weeks after the nephew reaches his majority, the uncle dies without having given him the money May the nephew proceed against the uncle's estate?
Answer	Yes. The consideration in this case is that the nephew lived up to a bargain—something he might not have done had not the uncle promised him the money.
Question	An aunt tells her nephew: "I will give you $750 if you will promise to attend my funeral." He does. May he enforce his claim against the aunt's estate?
Answer	Yes, for the same reason as in the above example.
Question	Alice, a spinster, lives with her brother Tom. For six years Alice keeps house for Tom and cares for his small children, but receives no pay and nothing is said on the subject. After Tom's death, Alice puts in a claim against his estate for compensation for services as housekeeper. Can she recover?
Answer	No. Where one rendering such services is a member of the family, receiving support therein, the law presumes that such services are donated gratuitously.
Question	A father tells his son that if the latter will buy a certain factory, the father will contribute $5,000 towards the purchase price. Relying on this promise, the son buys the factory, but the father dies before making the payment. Can the father's promise be enforced against his estate?

Answer	Yes, since the son did something which he might not have done and would not have been obligated to do had he not relied on his father's promise.
Question	An uncle promises his nephew to pay the expenses of the latter's trip to California. The nephew, relying upon the promise, makes the trip, spending his own money. Upon the nephew's return, the uncle dies. Does the nephew have a claim against the estate for the expenses of the trip?
Answer	Yes. For the same reason as above.
Question	Three sons are the heirs at law of Johnson, who dies, leaving a will. Before the will is read, the three sons agree that they will share their father's estate equally, regardless of the terms of the will. Later, when the will is read, it is learned that Johnson left his entire estate to Tom, one of the sons, who now refuses to transfer any of the property to the other two. Can he be compelled to do so?
Answer	Yes. The consideration in this case is good. It rests on the chance of each heir to gain something from the agreement, as well as the chance to lose.
Question	Jim gives Tom an option on his ranch for thirty days. The option mentioned $5 as the consideration. During the option period, oil is discovered on the land and Jim now seeks to revoke the option. May he do so?
Answer	No. A dollar is an adequate consideration for an option for the purchase of real estate, according to the weight of authority. The happening of an unexpected event, the discovery of oil in this case, would not affect the option's validity.
Question	George gives Henry a thirty-day written option to purchase George's house for $5,000. George receives no money for the option. Within the thirty days, Henry notifies George that he is taking up the option and offers George the $5,000. George refuses to give Henry the deed. Must he?
Answer	Yes. The acceptance of the option while it is in force makes the agreement binding.
Question	You engage Smith to build a house, the last payment of $1,000 to be made "when the house is completed according to specifications." When the house is completed, you refuse to pay on the ground that the builder used a cheaper grade of paint than specified and that there are certain defects in the plumbing, due to carelessness of the workmen

	employed. The builder now sues you for the $1,000. Are you required to pay it?
Answer	Yes, but you may deduct a full allowance for the defects.
Question	Mrs. Smith goes into a department store to buy a hat. She tells the salesgirl that she wants to buy the hat, subject to the approval at her husband. The salesgirl agrees. Mr. Smith does not approve. Mrs. Smith returns the hat which is now refused by the salesgirl. Must Mrs. Smith keep the hat?
Answer	No. The hat was purchased conditionally and, Since the condition was not fulfilled, she may return the hat.
Question	In consideration of his wife's dismissing a suit for divorce against him, Brown agrees not to live with his mistress. He further stipulates that if in the future, he resumes relations with his mistress, he will convey certain real estate to his wife. Subsequently, Brown returns to his mistress. May the wife obtain the real estate promised by Brown?
Answer	Yes. This contract is binding because Brown's agreement not to live with his mistress is recognized in law as being good morals and sound public policy.
Question	Mrs. Brown engages an artist to paint her portrait, it being stipulated that the painting shall be to Mrs. Brown's satisfaction. After the portrait is completed, Mrs. Brown refuses payment on the ground that the painting is "not to her satisfaction." Must she pay the artist?
Answer	No. In this class of contracts, where the element of personal taste is involved, Mrs. Brown is the sole judge of whether or not the portrait is satisfactory. She may, therefore, arbitrarily declare her dissatisfaction and refuse payment.
Question	What is a "divisible" contract?
Answer	Under such a contract it is possible to repudiate separate units of the goods sold without being held liable for breach of the entire contract. In short, the person repudiating would not be bound to pay for any items rejected.
Question	From samples submitted, the Jones Company orders twelve dozen pairs of overalls at different prices for each dozen. When delivered, only one dozen pairs conform to the samples. These the Jones Company keeps, returning eleven dozen. The manufacturer now sues the Jones Company for the purchase price of the entire twelve dozen. Can he

recover?

Answer No. This is a divisible contract; therefore, the Jones Company can keep one lot and return the others.

Question What is an "indivisible" contract?

Answer This is a contract where the repudiation of any unit of the goods or merchandise sold makes the party so repudiating liable for the breach of the entire contract.

Question Jackson contracts to deliver six hundred tons of coal to Benson on October 12th and four hundred tons on October 22nd. Benson agrees to pay $1,500 on October 27th and $8,000 on November 15th. Jackson delivers the six hundred tons on October 12th, but refuses to deliver the four hundred tons on October 22nd. As a result, Benson refuses to make any payment at all. What are the rights of the parties?

Answer This is an indivisible contract, Jackson, when he failed to make the second delivery, breached the entire contract. When that breach occurred, the contract being indivisible, Benson could repudiate the entire agreement and need not pay Jackson for either the first installment of coal which was delivered, or the second installment which was not delivered.

Question Smith, by a written agreement, promises to deliver five thousand gallons of oil to Jones at seven cents per gallon. Subsequently, Smith delivers two thousand gallons of oil and demands payment. Jones refuses to pay until the balance of the oil is delivered. Must he do so?

Answer This is an indivisible contract. When Smith fails to deliver the five thousand gallons he forfeits right to secure payment for any part of the oil. According to agreement, it is five thousand gallons which are to be delivered, not two thousand, so Smith can only rightfully claim payment when he fulfills his share of the contract by delivering the five thousand gallons. Jones can retain the oil and sue Smith for breach of contract.

Question Fred writes Catharine as follows: "I do hereby promise Catharine that I will not marry any person except herself. If I do, I agree to pay to Catharine $1,000 within three months after I shall marry someone else." A year later, Fred does marry another woman and Catharine sues for breach of contract. Can she recover?

Answer No. Such agreements are illegal, being against public policy.

Question Mrs. Blunt, a widow, applies to a matrimonial agency in quest of a husband. She pays the agency an application fee of $50, signing a written agreement whereby she agrees to pay an additional $450 should a husband he provided within sixty days of the agreement. Within the stipulated time a husband is duly provided, and, after demand, Mrs. Blunt, now Mrs. Jones, refuses to pay the $450. Must she pay?

Answer No, not legally. Courts will not enforce such agreements, holding them to be contrary to public policy.

Question Mrs. Brown, age seventy, in consideration for being taken into an old age home, agrees to sign a contract whereby she turns over to the home all the property she then has and all that she may thereafter acquire. She is not in the home more than a few months when her brother dies, leaving her $2,000. Must she turn this money over to the home?

Answer No. Such an agreement is not binding on Mrs. Brown, it being unreasonable and against public policy.

Question I lend you money for the express purpose of gambling. You refuse to return what you owe me. Do I have a legal claim against you?

Answer Yes, the fact that the lender of money knows it will be used for illegal purposes, in this case gambling, does not prevent bias from recovering the amount loaned, according to the weight of authority. Courts take the view that, even though the lender knows the illegal purpose of the loan, he is not a party to the unlawful transaction.

Question John promises to pay Brown $500 if he will falsely testify in a divorce case. Brown so testifies, but John refuses to pay the money. Does Brown have a claim?

Answer No. Such a contract is void as being against public policy and good morals.

Question Tom owes Henry $200. Henry writes the following letter to Tom: "If you will send me $100 within one week, I will give you a release in full for my entire claim." Tom sends Henry a check for $100 within the week, but Henry fails to send Tom the promised release. Not only that, but Henry now sues Tom for the other $100. Can he recover?

Answer Yes. Henry is only getting back the money due him in the first place; he does not have to take less, despite his written promise to do so. This is only true, however, where the amount of the bill is undisputed.

Question Arthur owes Bill $500. In a letter to Arthur, Bill states that if Arthur will pay $350 within one week of the date of the letter, Bill will give him a release and discharge in full for his entire claim. Bill further stipulates in his letter that he will not claim lack of consideration for the release of the $150. Relying on the promises contained in Bill's letter, Arthur sends Bill a check for $350 marked "Paid in Full." A few days later, Bill tiles suit for the additional $150. Is he entitled to recover?

Answer   Yes. There is no legal consideration for Bill's offer to take $350 in full settlement for the $500 claim; Bill's agreement to discharge the balance needs some other consideration besides part payment of a debt which is undisputed. In this case, the debtor incurs no legal detriment and Bill, the creditor, is only getting what he is lawfully entitled to 1 thousand gallons. Jones can retain the oil and sue Smith for breach of contract.

Question   Fred writes, Catharine as follows: "I do hereby promise Catharine that I will not marry any person except herself. If I do, I agree to pay to Catharine $1,000 within three months after I shall marry someone else." A year later, Fred does marry another woman and Catharine sues for breach of contract Can she recover?

Answer   No. Such agreements are illegal, being against public policy

Question   Mrs. Blunt, a widow, applies to a matrimonial agency in quest of a husband; She pays the agency an application fee of $50, signing a written agreement whereby she agrees to pay an additional $450 should a husband be provided within sixty days of the agreement. Within the stipulated time a husband is duly provided and, after demand, Mrs. Blunt, now Mrs. Jones, refuses to pay the $450. Must she pay?

Answer   No, not legally. Courts will not enforce such agreements, holding them to be contrary to public policy.

Question   Mrs. Brown, age seventy, in consideration for being taken into an old age home, agrees to sign a contract whereby the turns over to the home all the property she then has and all that she may thereafter acquire. She is not in the home more than a few months when her brother dies, leaving her $2,000. Must she turn this money over to the home?

Answer   No. Such an agreement is not binding on Mrs. Brown, it being unreasonable and against public policy

Question   I lend you money for the express purpose of gambling You refuse to return what you owe me. Do I have a legal claim against you?

Answer   Yes. The fact that the lender of money knows it will be used for illegal purposes, in this case gambling, does not prevent him; from recovering the amount loaned, according to

Question   Your surgeon sends you a bill for $200 for an appended to my. No agreement is made beforehand as to the amount of the bill. You feel that $200 is more than you should pay and send your surgeon a check for $150, marked "Paid in Full." Your surgeon accepts the check, cashes it, then sends you another bill for $50. Do you have to pay?

Answer   Yes. Marking a check "Paid in Full," a common practice among debtors, has no legal value. However, in a case such as this where the amount is in dispute, marking a check "Paid in Full in re-disputed amount" will operate as a discharge of the obligation—if accepted and cashed.

Question   Tom turns over his house to Henry, a real estate broker, to sell. Henry finds a customer ready, willing and able to buy Tom's house at the agreed price and upon certain specified conditions. Tom now says that he has changed his mind about selling and refuses to go through with the deal. Henry sues Tom for the usual broker's commission. Must Tom pay it?

Answer   Yes. A broker is entitled to his commission when he secures a buyer ready, willing and able to buy on the owner's terms.

Question   Torn gives Charles the exclusive right for thirty days to sell Tom's property, promising to pay him a commission of five per cent of the selling price. Charles is about to close the deal with a prospective customer on the fifteenth day when Tom notifies Charles that he no longer wants Charles to represent him. What can Charles do?

Answer   He can file suit and recover the profits he would have made had he been allowed to proceed with the sale.

Question   At an auction sale at which John is present, the auctioneer offers a set of China dishes to the highest bidder John, offering the highest bid, receives the set. When he goes up to examine the set, he discovers that it is not the one which he thought was being auctioned. May he cancel the sale?

Answer   Yes. Where a man bids upon one lot of goods, supposing it to be another, he is not bound. Here, there is a mistake as to the thing being sold which will void the contract.

Question At an auction sale of land, the auctioneer verbally corrects an error in the printed advertisement of the sale. Harry is present at the sale but does not hear the correction. He buys the land, supposing that he is buying the property as advertised. May he cancel the sale when he later learns that the land does not conform to the printed advertisement?

Answer Yes. Since the auctioneer has reference only to the corrected advertisement and the buyer to the uncorrected one, legally their minds have not met as to what is being sold; hence, Harry may cancel the sale.

Question Peter owns a blooded cow and is trying to sell the animal to George. Both Peter and George believe the cow to be barren, and Peter agrees to sell her for $80. If the cow could breed, she would be worth $1,000. After the bill of sale is signed, the cow is discovered to be with calf, and Peter now seeks to cancel the contract. May he do so?

Answer Yes. No sale would have taken place except upon the understanding and belief that the cow was barren. When parties contract under a mutual mistake as to the respective rights, the contract may be set aside as not reflecting the real intention of the parties.

Question John and George are negotiating for the sale of fifty crates of oranges, but no agreement is reached. John sends a telegram to George reading, "Send me three crates." The telegram, as delivered, reads, "Send me the crates," and George ships the fifty crates. Is John bound to accept fifty crates?

Answer No. John is not bound by the altered telegram. Since there has been no meeting of the minds, there is no contract.

Question There is an agreement to buy a lot in Walnut Street. It appears that there are two streets by that name, the buyer is intending to purchase a lot on one of said streets, and the seller to sell a lot on the other. Can this contract be enforced?

Answer No. This agreement is void because of a mistake as to the identity of the subject matter

Question In buying a cigar Larry gives the storekeeper a coin which he and the dealer suppose to be a half dollar, but which is really a gold coin valued at ten dollars. May Larry later recover the gold coin?

Answer Yes. Here the mistake is as to the quality of the thing—to wit, the value of the coin, and this makes the sale void.

Question Two men negotiate for the sale of a mule. John believes he is selling the mule for $16 and Bill is equally honest in the belief that he is buying it for $6, he takes the mule away. Later, John seeks to have the sale cancelled. Can he?

Answer Yes. This is a mistake as to the price. Where such a mistake exists, there is no contract since the minds of the parties have not met.

Question You own a cow which you know is diseased. You sell the cow to George, but make no mention of the cow's disability. Later, when. George learns about it, he wishes to cancel the contract and recover his money. May he do so?

Answer Yes. Such a concealment amounts to fraud; it enables the party victimized to cancel the contract at his option.

Question Jones looks at some land and, after Williams assures him that it is of good quality, buys it. Later, when Jones discovers, that the land is not as fertile as he expected, he sues to cancel the sale and recover the installments paid on the purchase price May he do so?

Answer No assertions of value or quality, when not warranted or guaranteed, though false, are not fraudulent. Such statements are mere matters of opinion. Hence, Jones will be bound by his contract

Question Arthur, upon retiring from business, offers to sell his adding machine to Brown for $200. Arthur states that he paid $300 for the machine and that its use in Brown's business will save him the expense of a bookkeeper Arthur knows that his statement is false-that he paid only $200 for the machine. Brown buys it for $200. May Brown cancel the contract when he later discovers that Arthur only paid $200?

Answer Yes. Representations as to cost are not matters of opinion and therefore may constitute fraud or misrepresentation. Where a contract is rendered unfair .by fraud or misrepresentation, it may be avoided by the defrauded party.

Question A mother promises a bystander $1,000 if he will rescue her child from drowning. The child is saved. Can the stranger obtain the $1,000 when the mother refuses to give it to him?

Answer   No. Agreements made while acting under stress and excitement may be repudiated.

Question The Alaskan Ice Company furnishes ice to Jackson under an agreement whereby Jackson pays $6.50 per ton for all the ice he uses during the year. The Alaskan Ice Company sells its business to another ice company which continues to supply ice to Jackson—who believes he is still buying from the original dealer. When, at the end of the year, Jackson receives a bill from the second ice company, he refuses to pay on the ground that he only dealt with the Alaskan concern. Is Jackson justified in refusing to pay?

Answer   No. The sale of the business to the second concern, together with the conduct of the Alaskan Ice Company in permitting the other ice company to fill such orders, indicates an assignment of the Alaskan's contract to the other ice' company. Hence, when the second company carries out and performs the orders actually received, it has the rights of an assignee and, may recover from Jackson.

Question John sells his grocery store to Bill. Before buying it, however, Bill gets John to sign an agreement that John will not open another grocery store within ten blocks of the old one for a period of five years. A year after John sells his store, he opens one five blocks away What can Bill do about it?

Answer   He can sue John for breach of contract and collect damages. In order to be binding, an agreement such as above must be reasonably related to the protection of the business sold This one does appear to be reasonable, and so Bill has a right of action

Question You sell your filling station, agreeing not to Open another one anywhere in the city for a period of three years. Within six months, you open one five miles away from the original one. Suit is brought against you for breach of contract. What will the court decide?

Answer   Probably, that you have not committed a breach of contract, since the stipulation not to open a filling station anywhere in the city would be considered unreasonable. The fact that the new filling station is not near enough to the old one to affect its business would also tend to decide the ease in your favor.

Question Jackson and King enter into a written agreement. By its terms Jackson agrees to employ King for one year at $5,000 There is an oral agreement between the parties that King is to "kick back" $20 per week. May this oral agreement be later introduced at the trial when Jackson sues King for breach of contract?

Answer No. Neither party to a contract may seek to vary its written terms by offer of proof of an oral agreement. Hence, oral evidence will not be admitted to show that a promise contained in a written contract is not the actual promise made by the parties.

Question You are employed to clean and repair a number of framed pictures for which service Adams agrees to pay you a certain price. After you have worked on a few of the pictures, Adams cancels the order. Nevertheless, you go ahead and complete all the work originally given you. You sue for the full price. Can you recover?

Answer You can only recover for the work performed by you prior to the cancellation of the order.

Question Arthur agrees to deliver to Brown an air conditioning limit for $2,000 within sixty days. Brown. agrees to pay $2,000 within one year from date of delivery, giving him a promissory note. When the time for delivery arrives, Brown is insolvent. Arthur knows this and, instead of delivering the air conditioning unit to Brown, sells it to Thompson for $2,000. The unit is actually worth $2,500, and Brown sues Arthur for $500. Can he recover?

Answer No. Brown's insolvency does not cancel the contract, but merely relieves Arthur of the necessity of extending credit If Brown had tendered the cash, Arthur would have been bound, despite his insolvency. Since, at the time of the in solvency, Brown could not tender cash, Arthur is justified in selling the unit to another.

Question You employ Mr. Downs, a nonresident, to come to your city as manager of one of your stores. It is agreed in writing that he is to assume his duties as of June 1st. Without notifying you he arrives June 8th, whereupon you inform him that the contract is cancelled. Mr. Downs sues you for breach of contract Can he recover?

Answer If Downs' delay was due to illness or any other circumstances over which he had no control, he could probably recover damages. However, if the delay was deliberate and without sufficient excuse, causing great loss and convenience, he probably could not recover.

Question An owner of a grain elevator agrees to receive a certain quantity of grain. When he receives the grain, the owner funds the storage capacity of this elevator has been taken up by other parties. Is the owner liable for breach of contract?

Answer Yes. The owner will not be excused from performance.

Question A contract provides that Jones shall drive logs down a stream to a certain river. Before Jones has time to do so, the water in the stream suddenly falls and remains so low that further performance of the contract is made impossible. Is Jones liable?

Answer No. He is excused from performance, since the contract does not contemplate that Jones shall transport the logs in any way except down the stream.

Question A house is blown down by a hurricane while 1n the course of erection. Upon whom does the loss fall?

Answer On the contractor who agreed to erect it. He is under an obligation to rebuild. The owner of the land is under an equal obligation to permit him to rebuild.

Question A store is leased for the sale of intoxicating liquors. A few months later, a statute is enacted prohibiting the sale of liquor. The tenant now seeks to cancel his contract May he do so?

Answer Yes. The above case is an illustration of a contract discharged because of a "legal impossibility." Where this occurs, the contract is cancelled.

Question Phillips, a contractor, agrees in writing to construct a dwelling for Smith for $8,500. The next day, Phillips suffers a heart attack. Is he excused from performing the contract?

Answer No. The law takes the view that he himself need not actually do the work but can secure others to do it for him. Therefore, he is not relieved of responsibility.

Question Frank employs a contractor to build a house, agreeing to pay him $5, 000. After building a portion of it, the contractor is taken ill and is unable to complete the job. Is the comma tor excused from further performance?

Answer No, for the same reason as above. In this case, the con« tractor is entitled to be paid for the part performed, if done properly, but Frank may deduct damages If or the breach of contract.

Question   Black agrees to let the Women's Club have the use of his music hall for a concert on a certain day. Before the day of performance arrives, the music hall is destroyed by fire. The Women's Club thereupon sues Black for breach of contract. Will recovery be permitted?

Answer   No. This contract is subject to an implied condition that the parties shall be excused in case performance becomes impossible, due to destruction. of the thing involved, in this case the music hall. Black would not be liable for breach of contract.

Question   A famous pianist is engaged by a concert bureau to give a recital. The night of the concert the musician is unable to play, due to a severe cold. The concert' bureau has gone to considerable expense in issuing tickets, advertising, etc. and files suit against the pianist for breach of contract. Can it recover?

Answer   No, unless the parties expressly agreed that incapacity due to' illness, transportation difficulties, etc. should not excuse. Where the contract is silent as to this point, no recovery is

possible. The principle of law is that where the performance, relates to personal services which can only be rendered by the person promising to perform them, the death or serious illness of that person will excuse performance and hence will relieve him of liability in a suit for breach of contract.

Question   How is a contract discharged?

Answer   1. By agreement of the parties before a breach of the contract has taken place.

2. By substituting a new contract in place of the old one.

3. By inserting in the contract a provision. which causes the agreement to be extinguished upon the happening of some event.

4. By performing the contract.

5. By impossibility of performance of the contract.

6.By cancellation of the contract for some defect such as fraud, mistake or undue influence.

7.By a breach of the contract by one party so as to avoid the necessity of performance by the other party.

8.By the alteration of a written contract by one party without the consent of the other.

9.By a discharge in bankruptcy or insolvency.

Question   When is time considered to be the essence of a contract?

Answer   In business contracts, stipulations as to the time when an act shall be performed are generally of the essence-for example, where a contract stipulates that one hundred fall suits are to be, delivered by September 1st and they are delivered September 5th, the buyer need not accept, them. Time may be made the essence of a contract by the express stipulation of the parties, or it may be construed to be such from the nature of the transaction.

Question   Doherty agrees to convey his farm to Peterson. Peterson agrees to pay $10,000 for it on July 15th. On July 17th, Peterson tenders the money to Doherty who refuses to accept. Can Peterson secure the farm on July 17th?

Answer   Yes. Since time was not made the essence of the contract, a few days' delay will not affect the validity of the agreement. By tendering the money on July 17th, Peterson can enforce the contract.

Question   Brown employs Smith and Company to build a house for him, agreeing to pay $10,000. After laying the foundation and erecting the framework, the builders, willfully and without legal excuse, abandon the project. Is Brown under any obligation to pay Smith and Company for the work already done?

Answer   No. Brown can either sue Smith and Company for breach of contract, or employ another builder to complete the job, charging Smith and Company with the difference.

Question   John is employed as a clerk by Mr. Jones to run a branch grocery store for three years. Mr. Jones dies during the second year of the written contract. Is John entitled1to recover wages for the unexpired portion of the agreement?

Answer   No. The death of the employer puts an end to the contract. This applies only to contracts, however, where personal services are involved.

Question   John is employed in a shoe store as a salesman, receiving a weekly salary. A few months later, John is discharged because of incompetency, receiving his discharge on a Wednesday. John claims he is entitled to be paid for the entire week. His employer claims that John need be paid only up to and including Wednesday. Who is right?

Answer   The employer. When a servant or employee is rightfully discharged, he need only be paid his wages to date.

Question   Suppose, in the above case, John is wrongfully discharged.

To What is he entitled?

Answer   He may recover his entire weekly salary. John must, however, seek other employment to minimize damages This means that he must attempt, in good faith, to obtain another job. If, for example, he is discharged on a Wednesday, makes a. bona tide attempt to get another job and fails to do so, his employer will owe him salary for the full Week. Should John find another job on Friday and begin work that day, his former employer will owe him salary, only from Monday through Thursday.

Question   Smith defaults on a certain contract he made with Brown. Smith. agrees to pay Brown $2, 500 in full satisfaction of the breach. Subsequent to this agreement, but before Smith pays any part of the $2, 500, Brown sues Smith for the original breach of contract, claiming $6, 000 damages Does Brown have a valid claim?

Answer   Yes. When there is an agreement to cancel an old claim, it is conditioned upon the new agreement being fully executed by performance. So long as there is no performance under the new agreement, the old one remains in effect. Hence, the failure of Smith to pay any portion of the $2,500 restores to Brown all the rights he had under the original agreement, including the right to sue for breach of contract for the full $6,000.

Question   Bill meets Jackson and orally offers him $10,000 for his farm. Jackson accepts his offer. Bill gives Jackson $1,000 to seal the bargain, agreeing to pay the balance the next day. Jackson accepts the offer and tells Bill he will give him a deed the following day. The next morning, Jackson tenders the deed, but Bill refuses to complete the transaction and demands his deposit back. Can Bill recover his deposit?

Answer   No. The above contract is one which must be in writing. Normally, one who pays money under an agreement condemned by the statute of frauds, as in the above case, is entitled to the return of the money so paid. To obtain such a recovery it is essential that the one seeking the return of the deposit be ready, willing and able to complete his share of the bargain. This Bill refuses to do when he fails to pay the balance and complete the purchase. And, since Bill repudiated the contract, he cannot recover his deposit.

Advisory 3

AGENCY

There was a time, not so many years ago, when the average business man ran his establishment entirely alone. With the growth and expansion of business it became increasingly difficult for one man to handle a variety of complex jobs. More and more he found it expedient to delegate power and responsibility to others. He began to appoint agents to act in his stead, investing them with authority to make binding contracts in his name.

Today, most of us, in one way or another, are either agents or employ others to act as agents for us. A salesman in a store is an agent for the owner. A real estate broker who is authorized to sell your house is your agent. An insurance man acts on behalf of his company.

The law of agency deals with the scope or extent of an agent's authority. Very often, the extent of that authority is not clearly defined, since there is no written instrument to serve as a guide. Hence it follows that, in most cases, the authority must be implied from the circumstances in each case, with special reference to previous custom either between the parties or in the particular trade or business. Conflicts commonly arise when the principal alleges that the agent exceeded his authority or that he never had the authority to act in the first place.

Agency deals with other matters as well. It is concerned, for example, with the duties and obligations of the agent to his principal, and, conversely, with the duties and obligations of the principal to his agent. Since there comes a time when the principal or agent seeks to end the relationship, the subject deals with the way agency may be terminated by either of the parties.

Question   What is agency?

Answer   An agency is a contractual relationship between two or more persons by which one party, called the agent, undertakes to perform certain acts for and on behalf of the other party, called the principal.

Question How is an agency created?

Answer An agency may be created orally, by written instrument, or implied by the circumstances or behavior of the parties

Question What is a principal?

Answer A principal is one who, being himself legally competent to do any act for his own benefit or on his own account, entrusts it to another person to do for him.

Question What is an agent?

Answer An agent is one who undertakes to transact some business by the authority and for the account of another.

Question Paul employs Arthur to obtain photographs illustrating Indian life. Arthur finds it necessary, in order to obtain such photographs, to employ an interpreter and to make small gifts to the Indians in order to induce them to have such photographs taken. Does Arthur have authority to employ an interpreter and procure gifts so as to make Paul, the principal, liable?

Answer Yes. Unless otherwise agreed, authority to conduct a transaction includes authority to do acts which are incidental to it, usually accompany it, or are reasonably necessary to accomplish it.

Question Bill employs Jack to sell goods in a farming community in which such goods are commonly sold on six months' credit. Jack, the agent, knows that Bill's goods there and elsewhere have been sold only on thirty days' credit. Does Jack, the agent, have authority to sell on six months' credit?

Answer No. An agent is authorized to comply with business customs only if the principal has notice that such customs exist. However, even usage or established business customs cannot contradict the specific terms of the known desires of the principal.

Question Paul employs Arthur to open a store for him on June 1st. Under such a general agreement, what is Arthur empowered to do?

Answer He may make arrangements for employing assistants and obtaining merchandise in anticipation of the opening, along with any other acts incidental td the opening of the store. However, Arthur is not authorized to sell merchandise in the store prior to June 1st.

Question Jim employs Charles to manage Jim's grocery store. In Jim's absence, Charles contributes $50 of the store's money to The Community Chest, to which merchants generally contribute. Does Charles have authority to do this so as to make Jim liable?

Answer Yes. Unless otherwise agreed, authority to act as agent includes only authority to act for the benefit of the principal. Charles' contribution to The Community Chest is for Jim's benefit, as it obtains or retains good will.

Question Paul employs a real estate broker to find a purchaser for Paul's house at a stated price. Does the real estate broker have authority to contract for its sale?

Answer No. Authority to contract is not inferred from authority to solicit business for the principal, nor from authority to perform acts of service for the principal.

Question Paul appoints Arthur as his agent to remodel his house according to specifications supplied by Paul. Does Arthur have authority to make contracts with artisans and those selling building materials, so as to bind Paul?

Answer Yes. Unless otherwise agreed, authority to make a contract is inferred from authority to conduct a transaction, if the making of such a contract is incidental to the transaction, usually accompanies it, or is reasonably necessary to accomplish it. In this case, in order to remodel the house Arthur must procure the necessary materials and workers. Hence, Paul will be bound.

Question A steel company authorizes Jack to establish. and construct a permanent branch of its steel mills. Nothing is Specifically said about the acquisition of a site. Does Jack have the authority to acquire the necessary land so as to make the steel company liable?

Answer Yes, for the same reason as in Question 10.

Question Paul appoints Henry as the general manager of Paul's farm, upon which stock, grain and fruits are raised for sale. Does Henry have authority to sell the products of the farm?

Answer Yes. Henry's contract calls for raising crops for sale. Therefore, he has the implied power to-sell those crops.

Question Jim authorizes Harry to go about the country selling Jim's goods. Jim puts into Harry's possession several large packages of goods and samples, but makes no provision for transporting them except by railroad. It is necessary to transport the goods and samples from one part of a city to another. Does Harry have authority to hire a taxicab to convey the samples and to charge the. expense to Jim?

Answer Yes. Authority to buy or sell usually includes authority .to secure such assistance as the proper performance of the transaction requires.

Question Paul appoints Arthur as his manager to operate several coal mines and to ship the coal to a seaport. Arthur finds that one of the mines cannot be operated profitably and wishes to sell it. May he do so?

Answer No. Authority to conduct a business does not include authority to sell the business.

Question Paul authorizes Alan to sell and convey a large farm to a "satisfactory buyer for $5,000." Alan sells and conveys the farm for $4,000 in money, with a mortgage for $1,000. After the conveyance is made, Paul seeks to have the sale set aside Will he succeed?

Answer Yes. Alan had no authority to make such terms. Unless otherwise agreed, authority to sell includes only authority to sell for money payable at the time of the transfer of title. It does not include authority to mortgage the subject matter, to exchange it, to make a gift of it, or to grant an option of purchase.

Question Arthur is a traveling salesman for Paul, a wholesale grocer. On one of his trips, Arthur obtains from Tom an order for goods which he sends to Paul. Paul accepts the order and sends the goods to Tom. On his next trip, Arthur again visits Tom who pays Arthur the amount due on the goods previously sold. Arthur then absconds with the money. Paul now seeks to hold Tom liable. Will he succeed?

Answer Yes. Arthur was not authorized to receive such payment; Tom will be liable to Paul if he makes payment to Arthur. An agent is not authorized to receive payment unless he is expressly given power to do so by his principal. When a third party, in this case Tom, pays the agent rather than the principal, he does so at his own risk.

Question Paul employs Jim as an auctioneer to sell his horse. Jim sends the horse to another auctioneer to sell. May Jim legally do this?

Answer No. The first auctioneer has no authority to delegate his job to the second auctioneer, and the second auctioneer has no authority to, sell the horse. Unless otherwise agreed, authority to conduct a transaction does not include authority to delegate to another the performance of acts incidental there to which involve discretion or the agent's special skill.

Question   Paul tells his wife that she may open charge accounts with certain designated local stores, but with no others. In Paul's name, the wife opens accounts with the designated stores and also with others, the latter accounts not being revealed to Paul. Small bills for supplies are incurred. Each month Paul gives his wife the money to pay the household bills, making no inquiries as to the creditors. At the end of six months, Paul. discovers the facts and refuses to pay the current bills of the unauthorized stores. May these stores recover from Paul?

Answer   Yes. A wife has apparent authority to incur such indebtedness, since the husband is under a legal obligation to support and supply his wife with the necessaries for her existence.

Question   Paul, a peach grower, ships peaches to his factor (commission merchant) in the city; Twelve hours before they are due to arrive, the factor learns that in his city, owing to excessive arrivals, peaches will not bring enough to satisfy the freight charges, but that, if diverted to a factor in another city, the peaches will bring a much higher price at no greater freight cost. He does divert them, but the peaches are unexpectedly destroyed by flood. Is the factor liable?

Answer   No. He is authorized to re-route the fruit; the fact that it may be unexpectedly destroyed by flood in the other city does not subject him to liability to the principal. Unless otherwise agreed, an agent may do what he reasonably believes to be necessary in order to prevent substantial loss to the principal.

Question   Paul owns a store. He marks the sale price of his goods in a cipher which the clerks understand, and directs them to sell the goods at those prices. A customer applies to one of these clerks for an article, inquiring as to the price. The clerk, mistakenly reading the cipher, names a price lower than the one marked. The customer buys the article, paying the clerk the price named. Is Paul, the owner, bound by this sale?

Answer   Yes. The clerk was acting within the apparent scope of his authority.

Question   A fire insurance company appoints Arthur as its general agent for a certain state. It is agreed that Arthur open offices in cities selected by him and receive a commission on business done. Does Arthur have power to appoint subagents?

Answer   Yes. And the subagents, by their authorized acts, may bind the company. A general agent has either express or implied authority to appoint subagents. The authority is expressed when the principal, in writing or otherwise, gives the general agent such authority. This authority is implied when the exigencies of a business, as in the present case, compel the general agent to appoint subagents to help in carrying on that business. A subagent, employed without the knowledge or consent of the principal, has a remedy against his immediate employer only. As against the latter, the subagent has the Same rights, obligations and duties as if the agent were the sole principal. However, where a subagent is ordinarily or necessarily employed in a business, as in the present example, he can maintain a claim for compensation both against the principal and the immediate employer, unless exclusive credit is given the principal—in which case his remedy is against the principal only.

Question   Paul directs Arthur to make a written contract in Paul's name for the purchase of goods. Arthur buys goods from Thompson who knows that Arthur is acting for Paul, the memorandum specifying that Arthur is the buyer. Is Paul subject to liability on the contract?

Answer   Yes. A principal who directs an agent to make a contract in the principal's name is subject to liability, although made in the agent's name, unless the principal is excluded from it by its terms.

Question   The Perkins Company employs Jack to sell shares in the company, instructing Jack not to make any representations except those contained in the prospectus. The prospectus is silent concerning the assets of the company, the number of shareholders or the company's affiliations. Jack makes false statements concerning the assets of the company upon which Thompson, a buyer, relies. Jack contracts with Thompson by a written agreement in which it is stated that Jack is not authorized to make statements except those in the prospectus. May Thompson repudiate the agreement when he learns of Jack's false statements, and hold the Perkins Company liable?

Answer   Yes. Although a principal tells an agent that the agent is not authorized to make particular statements, if he believes the agent will make such statements and that they will be relied upon by persons with whom the agent deals, the principal will be held liable.

Question   Paul, a manufacturer, who has previously done his own buying, appoints Arthur as purchasing agent, telling him that he is to buy what the mill needs. During his first three months, Arthur purchases coal of a grade not previously used in the mill. Paul pays the monthly bills for this, knowing of the change. Later he changes his mind and seeks to have the orders cancelled. May he do so?

Answer   No. By paying the bills with knowledge of the change, Paul has affirmed Arthur's conduct and bound himself thereby.

Question   In the absence of Bill, the owner and manager of a small newspaper, his friend Arthur takes charge, without authority, and publishes several issues. In the course of these he libels Tom. On Bill's return, he affirms the publication. May Tom recover damages from Bill?

Answer   Yes. Bill has ratified Arthur's originally unauthorized act, by doing so he makes himself responsible for Arthur's libel of Tom.

Question   Pretending to act for Paul, but actually without power to do so, Arthur contracts to purchase goods from Thompson. Upon learning of the transaction, Paul writes Thompson that he will have nothing to do with the deal. While Thompson is wondering what to do with the goods, he receives a letter from Paul stating that he wishes the goods. Is Paul now bound to accept them?

Answer   Yes. He has ratified a previously unauthorized act; by doing so he makes himself liable.

Question   Jim appoints Henry as sales manager; Henry affirms for Jim unauthorized contracts made by Jim's salesmen before Henry's appointment. May Henry legally do this?

Answer   Yes. An agent may be authorized to ratify for his principal the previous unauthorized acts of another agent.

Question   Arthur, a clerk employed by Paul, but having nothing to do with advertising, places an advertising order for six months with Tom, in Paul's name. Paul learns of this and, although he knows that Tom is preparing copy, does nothing about it. Is

Paul liable for the unauthorized act of Arthur?

Answer   Yes. Confirmation of an unauthorized transaction may be implied from a failure to repudiate it.

Question   Jim asks Charles to buy fifty tons of coal for him. Charles buys the coal from Tom through correspondence, not revealing, however, that he is acting for a principal. Who is liable for the coal?

Answer   Jim. He is what is called an undisclosed principal. Such a principal is bound by contracts made on his accounts by an agent acting within his authority.

Question   Peter directs Anthony to buy goods in Anthony's name, Peter alone to be responsible to the seller. In order to carry out his agreement with Peter, Anthony, in contracting with Tom, refuses to divulge whether he is acting for himself or for a principal. He includes in the contract a provision that he alone shall be subject to liability. After Anthony repudiates the contract, Tom, the seller, learns that Peter is the principal and seeks to hold him liable. Can he?

Answer   No. An undisclosed principal does not become liable on a contract which provides that he shall not be a party to it.

Question   Arthur offers to contract with Tom, but Tom refuses to deal with him. Arthur then falsely represents that he is acting as agent for another whose name he does not disclose. A contract is made, Arthur signing the document "Arthur, Agent." Is Arthur liable, in case of default?

Answer   Yes. Where the real principal pretends to be an agent dealing for an unidentified principal, the fact that the other party is willing to deal with him does not prevent the fictitious agent from being liable when he is discovered to be the principal.

Question   Sam, acting for Paul but pretending to be acting wholly on his own account, contracts with Tom for one hundred bushels of grain, signing the memorandum with his name only. Who is liable in the event of default?

Answer   Paul; An undisclosed principal may be liable upon a contract in writing even though it purports to be the contract of the agent.

Question   Paul directs Arthur to shoot any unknown person entering premises belonging to Paul. Arthur shoots Tom who is rightfully entering the premises. Is Paul liable?

Answer   Yes. Paul is liable because he should have instructed Arthur not to shoot those lawfully entering the premises. By not doing so, he becomes liable for Arthur's wrongful act.

Question   Paul directs Arthur to use an automobile which, as Paul, knows but Arthur does not know, has a hidden defect, making the car dangerous. Owing to this defect, Arthur, while using the car, injures a pedestrian. Is Paul, the owner, liable?

Answer   Yes. Liability is based on the fact that Paul had knowledge of the defect which he failed to disclose to Arthur.

Question   Paul employs Carl to dig a hole in the street, instructing him to protect travelers therefrom. Carl digs the hole but fails to illuminate it. Tom, a pedestrian, is injured when he falls into the hole, owing to the absence of light. Is Paul liable?

Answer   Yes. A principal who is under a duty to provide protection for, or to have care used to protect others or their property, and who delegates the performance of such duty to an agent, is subject to liability for harm caused by the failure of such agent to perform the duty.

Question   Paul employs Burt to operate the former's grocery store in Burt's name. Burt employs clerks who believe that Burt is the actual owner. One of the clerks gets into a fight with a customer, severely injuring him. Is Paul liable?

Answer   Yes. An undisclosed principal is liable for conduct within the scope of employment of servants employed for him by an agent empowered to do so.

Question   Robert operates a small store and employs two clerks and a delivery boy. One of the clerks, during the absence of Robert and the delivery boy, although his ordinary employment does not include such service, delivers a package to a point close to the store, using a bicycle supplied for the delivery boy is use. While doing so, the clerk carelessly runs over a small boy. Is Robert liable?

Answer   Yes. The clerk is acting within the scope of his apparent authority.

Question   In selling guns, Jack directs his salesman never to insert a cartridge while exhibiting a gun. The salesman fails to follow this instruction and causes a gun to go off, killing a passer-by. Is Jack liable?

Answer   Yes. Even a forbidden act may be within the scope of the agent's or servant's authority. A master cannot direct a servant to accomplish a result, anticipating that he will always use the means which he directs or that he will refrain from acts which it is natural to expect that a servant may do.

Question Paul, the owner of a house, tells his janitor to collect the rubbish and to deposit it only in barrels provided for that purpose. The janitor, however, in collecting the rubbish, burns it in a vacant lot back of the house. Because of this, the house next door is set on fire. The owner naturally seeks to hold Paul liable. Can he do so?

Answer Yes, for the same reason as in Question 38.

Question Arthur, Paul's chauffeur, while on an errand for Paul, to avoid a rough spot in the road unlawfully drives upon the sidewalk, striking and injuring a pedestrian. Is Paul liable?

Answer Yes. Arthur was still acting within the scope of his authority.

Question Robert employs Jim as a watchman to guard against fires and burglaries. Jim discovers a fire which endangers Tom's house, but fails to put it out or to give the alarm in time. Tom's house burns down. Suit is filed against Robert. Will recovery be permitted?

Answer Yes. When Jim failed to give the alarm in time to prevent the fire from spreading, he was negligent and the principal or master will be held liable in damages.

Question Paul employs Arthur as a clerk. After the ordinary closing time, Arthur remains to clean some implements for the next day's use. In doing so he turns on and neglectfully fails to shut off water which, overflowing the bowl, runs into the apartment of a tenant on the door below. Is Paul liable?

Answer Yes. Arthur's failure to shut off the water is conduct within the scope of employment for which the principal is held liable.

Question Arthur, agent for an insurance company, employs a subagent, this being authorized; Arthur falsely represents' to the subagent that a rule of the company requires a cash deposit of $750. The subagent deposits this amount with Arthur who steals it. The subagent now seeks to recover the money from the insurance company. Can he?

Answer Yes. A principal who places an agent in a position enabling the latter, while apparently acting within his authority, to commit a fraud on another person is subject to liability for the fraud.

Question An automobile club authorizes Arthur to direct travelers. A traveler relies upon Arthur's statement that a particular road is safe; by doing so, the motorist is injured. Is the auto club liable?

Answer   Yes. The traveler has a right to rely on Arthur's statement, since Arthur was acting within his employment, even though he carelessly gave erroneous information.

Question Paul directs Arthur, a traveling salesman supplied with a car, to sell goods only in Albany. The salesman, however, drives to Rochester to sell goods: While driving there, he negligently injures a pedestrian. Suit is filed against Paul. Is he liable?

Answer   No. He is not liable since Arthur went an unreasonably long distance away from the place where he was authorized to do business. Hence, Arthur's acts in Rochester were not within the scope of his employment.

Question Bill is employed as a truck driver, with hours from eight to five. At four o'clock he finds he has a load to deliver. Instead of delivering it, he drives home, remaining there until ten o'clock, after which he delivers the load. While doing so he negligently injures a pedestrian. Is the truck owner liable?

Answer   No. Bill was not acting within the scope of his authority when he made the delivery at ten o'clock. Only Bill himself could be held liable, not the owner of the truck.

Question Arthur, a truck driver for Bill, invites Tom to ride with him, this being against orders. While Tom is riding with Arthur's consent, Arthur drives the truck at an excessive rate of speed to make up for lost time, causing an accident in which Tom is injured. Is Bill, the employer, liable?

Answer   No. Arthur had no authority to accept Tom as a passenger. When he did so, he himself assumed the legal obligation.

Question A shirt manufacturer employs Arthur, for a period of live years, as a traveling salesman to sell shirts on commission. Two years later, the factory burns down and the manufacturer does not resume business. Is he liable to Arthur?

Answer   Yes. The destruction of the factory does not relieve the manufacturer of liability; however, no action against the manufacturer can take place until he has had 'a reasonable than to rebuild the factory.

Question Paul promises Arthur a commission if he will find a purchaser for Paul's land. Arthur advertises and the advertisement is seen by Tom who, in response thereto, goes directly to Paul, the deal taking place without Arthur's knowledge. Is Arthur entitled to his commission?

Answer   Yes. An agent, whose compensation is conditional upon his accomplishment of a specified result, is entitled to the agreed compensation if, and only if, he causes the result. Arthur's "ad" accomplished this.

Question   Paul lists his house with Arthur for sale. Arthur introduces Tom, who agrees to meet Paul's terms, except for one or two minor matters. Paul agrees to think the matter over until the next day. Paul then telephones Arthur, dismissing him and advising that the deal is off. The next day, Paul seeks Tom who now agrees to the terms upon which Paul had insisted the day before. Is Arthur entitled to his commission?

Answer   Yes. Paul terminated his relations with Arthur in bad faith. Arthur had secured a buyer ready, willing and able to purchase the property. Paul would be liable.

Question   Paul places goods in the hands of an auctioneer. The auctioneer sells some of them, but the proceeds are insufficient to pay all of his charges on the transaction. May the auctioneer retain the unsold goods as security for his charges?

Answer   Yes. An agent who receives possession of goods has a right to retain possession until the principal has paid him what is due on them.

Question   Paul appoints Arthur as his agent to sell goods in markets where the highest price Can be obtained. Instead, Arthur sells on a glutted market, obtaining a low price. A higher price would have been obtained in a near-by market had Arthur used care in securing information which was available to him. Is Arthur liable?

Answer   Yes. A paid agent must act with reasonable skill in his undertakings. When Arthur failed to obtain such information, he was not acting with reasonable skill and diligence.

Question   Paul employs Jack as a clerk to sell goods, his remuneration being a weekly salary. Nothing is said as to the manner of selling. Paul later directs Jack to sell the goods at such unreasonable prices that practically nothing can be sold. Is Jack obliged to obey?

Answer   Yes. He must follow instructions. Even if Jack sells nothing he is still entitled to his salary; as long as Paul is paying that salary Jack must obey orders.

Question Jim, the purchasing agent for a railroad, buys, for a fair price, twenty-five automobiles from Tom, who is going out of business. Grateful for Jim's favorable action, Tom gives Jim a gift of a car. May Jim, the agent, retain the automobile?

Answer No. Unless otherwise agreed, an agent who makes a profit in connection with transactions conducted by him on behalf of the principal is obliged to give up such profit to the principal.

Question Robert directs Arthur to buy shares for him "at the market." Arthur, a broker, has such shares on hand; and, unable to obtain them elsewhere, he conveys his shares to Robert at the market price. Within a few days, Robert changes his mind and desires to cancel the transaction. May he?

Answer Yes. Unless otherwise agreed, an agent must not deal with his principal as an adverse or hostile party. This rule exists to prevent a conflict of interests in agents whose duty it is to act solely for the benefit of their principals.

Question Paul employs Arthur, for a term of three years, as a salesman in a mercantile business. As part of the contract, Arthur promises not to compete with the employer in the same ion for two years after termination of the contract. Is Arthur bound by such an agreement?

Answer Yes. Such a restraint is reasonable and is considered a valid protection of the employer's interests.

Question Suppose, in the above example, Arthur agrees never to compete with the employer in the same town. Would Arthur be bound?

Answer No. Such a restraint is considered unreasonable.

Question Harry is employed by Charles to buy wheat for future delivery, Harry carelessly fails to purchase the wheat. Had he done so, Charles would have made a profit. Is Harry liable?

Answer Yes. He is liable to Charles for such profit, for, in failing to follow his principal's instructions, he has caused him damage for which the agent can be held liable.

Question How is an agency terminated?

Answer 1. By revoking the agent's authority. This may be done in writing, orally, or may be implied from the circumstances.
2. By the agent's renouncing his right to act for and on

behal of the principal.

3. By the insanity of the principal or agent.
4. By the bankruptcy of the principal.
5. By the death of the principal or agent.
6. By the extinction of the subject matter of the agency.
7. By the complete execution of the trust.

Question   Dan is run over in the street. He asks several bystanders to find a doctor for him. Arthur, Ben, Charles and Paul start to look for one. Before Arthur can obtain one, he sees Ben summon a physician, Does Arthur still have authority to find a doctor?

Answer   No. His authority ends when he sees Ben procure a physician, for he can then imply from the circumstances that no further aid is needed.

Question   Paul authorizes Arthur to buy a bicycle for him. Arthur knows that Paul desires to buy only one bicycle; he also knows that Paul has not authorized any other agent to buy one. Before Arthur has bought a bicycle, Paul himself buys one. Arthur has no notice of this. May Arthur go ahead and purchase the bicycle, making Paul liable?

Answer   Yes. In the absence of evidence to the contrary, an agent's authority is not terminated until he has accomplished the purpose for which he was employed or is notified of the termination of his employment by the principal.

Question   Paul writes Arthur, agent, on June Ist: "Do not act further for me." The letter should have been received by Arthur on June 3rd, but it is lost in the mail. On June 5th, Arthur acts for Paul. Is Paul, the principal, liable?

Answer   Yes, because Arthur had no notice of the cancellation of authority.

Question   Paul has a growing crop for which a supply of water is essential. During a drought, Paul authorizes Arthur to contract for irrigating the crop. Before Arthur has a chance to act, rain comes, making irrigation no longer necessary. Arthur knows this. May he still go ahead and contract for the irrigation?

Answer   No. Arthur's authority is ended. When an agent has notice of the terminating event, such as, in this case, the rain, he no longer has authority to continue acting on behalf of his principal. Indeed, the terminating event is equivalent to notice that the principal has ended the agent's authority to act on his behalf.

Question Bert directs Jim to sell a piece of land for $5,000 its approximate value. Jim is a real estate agent living in a town ten miles from the land. Oil is discovered near-by and the price readily obtainable for the land triples. A week or so later, Jim not having learned of this, as he would have had he been attentive to his business, sells the land to Thompson for $5,000. May Bert repudiate the sale?

Answer Yes. An agent's authority ends or is suspended when the agent knows, or should know, of the happening of an event or a change in conditions, from which he may reasonably infer that the principal does not consent to the further exercise of authority, or would not consent if he knew the facts.

Question Paul gives Arthur, a broker, the exclusive right to sell his farm. Later, Paul conveys the farm to Fred. Without notice of such conveyance, Arthur contracts to sell the farm to Thompson. Is such a sale binding on Paul?

Answer Yes. Where the principal intentionally destroys or conveys the subject matter, the agent's authority to bind the principal by a contract is not terminated until the agent receives notice.

Question Paul authorizes Arthur to purchase goods for the establishment of a business in a Latin American country. Before Arthur makes any purchases, a revolution occurs in the Latin American country and all property there is confiscated. May Arthur legally continue to make purchases for and on behalf of Paul, with a view to starting the business?

Answer No. The outbreak of war, of which the agent has notice, ends his authority. The conditions are so changed that he should infer that the principal, if he knew the facts, would no longer consent to have the agent act in his behalf.

Question In consideration of Arthur's agreement to advertise and give his best energies to the sale of a farm, its owner, Frank, grants Arthur a power of attorney, irrevocable for one year,
to sell it. At the end of three months, Frank informs Arthur that he revokes the latter's authority to sell. May he do so?

Answer Yes. But Arthur has a right of action against Frank for breach of his contract.

Question Bill authorizes Jim to sell Bill's grain and receive the price thereof. The next day, Bill tells Jim to give a thousand bushels of the grain to the Red Cross. May Jim still sell this one thousand bushels and collect the money?

Answer No. A principal may end the agency by conduct inconsistent with its continuance, as in the above example. He may also end the agent's authority when he retakes possession of the goods, or disposes of the subject matter or of his interest therein.

Question Paul employs Arthur, among others, to solicit and make sales in a certain specific territory. A rule strictly enforced by Paul, and known to Arthur, is that all canvassers must report back to Paul's office weekly, and must look at the bulletin board for changes in assignments. Paul posts a document on the board stating that Arthur is dismissed. Arthur does not see the document on the day he is required to look at the bulletin board. May Arthur continue to make sales so as to bind Paul?

Answer No. Arthur's authority is terminated the day the notice of dismissal is posted on the bulletin board. Had Arthur looked at the board as he was required to do, he would have learned about the dismissal.

Question Jones buys an option on a piece of land and authorizes Jack to sell it. Two hours before the expiration of the option, and while Jack is in the process of executing its sale to Thompson, Jones dies. What can Jack do about it?

Answer Nothing. The death of the principal terminates the authority of the agent.

Question Paul employs Arthur, a stock broker, to buy at the market 5,000 shares of stock in Arthur's name-but for Paul's account. Unknown to anyone, Paul dies, and, a few minutes thereafter; Arthur buys the shares. May Arthur hold Paul's estate liable?

Answer No. An agent's authority ends upon the death of the principal, although the agent has no means of knowing at the time that the principal has died.

Question Paul authorizes Arthur to employ Ben as Arthur's subagent. This is done. Soon after, Arthur dies. Is Ben still subagent?

Answer No. The death of the agent terminates the authority of the subagent.

Question A fire insurance company appoints Arthur as its general agent in a certain town, supplies him with a registry book in which to register policies issued by him, and equips him with blank policies and other supplies for use in the business. Later, the lire insurance company cancels Arthur's authority, but does not require him to surrender his commission as agent. It permits him to retain the registry book. and supplies. Thompson deals with Arthur in reliance upon the appearance of his Continued authority caused by the possession of, the documents, and without notice of the revocation. Is the fire insurance company liable to Thompson, whose house burns down shortly after he takes out a policy through Arthur?

Answer   Yes. The fire insurance company would be bound to Thompson, since the latter had no notice that Arthur's authority as agent had been terminated.

Question   Paul, who carries on business in Chicago, employs Bill as i his general agent. Thompson knows of the agency but has never dealt with Bill. Paul later revokes Bill's authority and publishes a statement to that effect in a Chicago newspaper. Thompson does not see the statement; he deals with Bill in accordance with and in reliance upon, the former agency. May Thompson hold Paul liable for the deal made with Bill?

Answer   No. Paul has given sufficient notice of revocation to Thompson by publishing such notice in the newspaper.

Question   Paul appoints Arthur as his agent to sell land to Tom. That night, unknown to anybody, Paul dies. The following morning, Arthur executes a contract of sale to Tom in Paul's name. Who is liable on the contract?

Answer   Arthur. His authority ended with the death of Paul.

Question   Paul employs Helen, a motion picture actress, who, in disobedience to Paul's orders and without excuse, remains away from the studio for one day, causing production of the film to be held up. May Paul discharge Helen?

Answer   Yes. A principal may discharge an agent, before the time fixed by the contract bf employment, when the agent commits such a violation of duty that her conduct constitutes a material breach of contract.

Question   Arthur, employed by Paul as his bookkeeper for a year, steals small sums from the cash drawer. Paul, knowing this, retains Arthur in his employ. May Paul later discharge Arthur for the original theft?

Answer   Yes.

Advisory 4

SALES

The law of sales deals with the rights and obligations of buyers and sellers of commodities. It is primarily concerned with the passing of title from the seller to the buyer so that ownership of the goods may be legally determined, for it is be real owner who must bear the loss in case of damage or destruction. The passing of title, therefore, transfers owner tip from the seller to the buyer.

In a sale, or contract of sale, as it is sometimes called, title passes immediately to the buyer. This means that where goods are damaged or destroyed after the sale is made, the loss falls on the buyer, even though the seller retains temporary possession of them. In a contract to sell, on the other hand, title is reserved in the seller, so that if articles are destroyed the seller must bear the loss—despite the fact that the articles may be in the possession of the prospective buyer. When a contract to sell is completed, title passes to the buyer who must bear any loss from that point on.

Another important distinction is that in a sale the buyer nay not only sue for breach of contract, but may insist on having the thing itself sold. In a contract to sell, since the buyer never had title in the first place, his only remedy is an action from breach of contract—not a right to possession of the thing sold.

Question   A buyer purchases one hundred cases of marshmallow cream. When the order arrives, he finds that ninety cases are good, nine are broken and one case is missing. The seller offers to allow the purchaser a credit for the missing case as well as for the nine broken ones. The buyer, however, refuses to accept any part of the shipment. Is he legally justified in doing so?

Answer   Yes. The delivery of goods in an unsound condition is the same as a delivery of goods of a different quality or character. Even though the deterioration is slight, or only one case out of a large number is unsound or missing and the seller is willing to allow full credit, the buyer may refuse delivery.

Question Jones agrees to sell Brown his horse. Before the actual sale takes place the horse dies, through no fault of Jones. 19 Jones liable to Brown?

Answer No. The destruction of the subject matter before title passes excuses performance. If the horse had died after title passed, the loss would be Brown's, even though Jones still had possession.

Question Jones agrees to sell Brown five hundred bushels of May wheat. No particular lot of wheat is specified as the subject matter of the sale. Jones has five hundred bushels of wheat on hand. Before the sale takes place, this five hundred bushels is destroyed. Is Jones still bound to deliver the five hundred bushels of wheat?

Answer Yes. In this case, the destruction does not relieve the seller, for he can still perform his agreement by selecting out of other stock, or by going upon the market to buy.

Question Jones agrees to sell Brown an automobile, the price to be fixed by White. Is this a good contract?

Answer Yes. Where no price is. mentioned, a reasonable sum will be implied.

Question Jones tells Brown that he will sell him a horse for $100. Brown says he will take the horse. It is arranged that Brown shall come next day to pay for and get the animal. Before Brown can pay the purchase price, the horse dies, through no fault of either party. Must Brown still pay for the animal?

Answer Yes. Unless a different intention appears, where there is an unconditional contract to sell specific goods in a deliverable state, the property or title. in the goods passes to the buyer when the contract is made. It is immaterial whether I the time of payment or the time of delivery, or both, are postponed.

Question Snodgrass sells Barrett all the lumber in a certain lumber yard, at an agreed price. It is understood that Barrett may remove the lumber at any time Within four months; but he must pay the purchase price before removal. A few months after the agreement is made, but before payment, the lumber is destroyed by fire. Upon whom does the loss fall?

Answer   On Barrett. Title to property passes when the parties so intend. Neither delivery nor payment are necessary to the passing of title. The general rule is that title passes at once when the goods are in a deliverable state and nothing remains to be done except payment and taking of possession.

Question Farmer Smith brings a live calf to Brown's slaughter house. It is agreed that the calf be sold and delivered to Brown at fifteen cents per pound dressed weight. The following night the calf dies, through no fault of anyone. May Farmer Smith recover the purchase price from Brown?

Answer   Yes. The above is an unconditional contract to sell specific goods In a deliverable state. Under such a contract title passes at the time the bargain is made, unless the parties indicate a contrary intention. The fact that payment is postponed is immaterial. Since title passed to Brown, risk of loss also falls on him; upon the death of the calf Farmer Smith may recover the purchase price of the animal.

Question Jones contracts for the sale of corn in cribs to Brown. Jones agrees to shell it, haul it to the grain elevator and there weigh it. While on the way to the elevator, the corn is destroyed. Is Brown liable for the corn?

Answer   No. Unless a different intention appears, where there is a contract to sell specific goods and the seller is to do something to the goods for the purpose of putting them in a deliverable shape, as in the present case, title does not pass until such thing is done.

Question You offer to sell your car to Harry for $500. Harry refuses to buy unless certain repairs are first made to the automobile. You authorize Harry to take the car to a garage, have the repairs made and deduct the amount of the bill from the $500. Harry agrees, removing the car to a garage for repairs. While being repaired, the car is destroyed by fire, due to the garage man's carelessness. Can you hold the garage man liable?

Answer   No. Title to the car passed to Harry. The rule is that when the seller is bound to do something to the goods, for the purpose of putting them in a deliverable state, title does not pass until such thing is done. This presumption would apply in the present example had you retained possession of the automobile. Harry, however, had possession and, since you parted with the car, you cannot maintain an action against the garage man. You can, however, hold Harry responsible for the purchase price of the automobile. Harry, in turn, being the legal owner, may recover against the garage man.

Question   Farmer Jones buys a stack of hay from Smith, it being agreed that twenty-five tons are to be retained by Smith. Before Smith can remove the twenty-five tons so retained, the entire stack is destroyed by fire. Who must bear the loss?

Answer   Smith. Title to goods does not pass until they are "ascertained." They are "ascertained" when they are sufficiently identified to be set aside. In the above example, Smith did not segregate the twenty-five tons of hay. Not having done so, the goods are "unascertained" and the loss is Smith's.

Question   Jones, wishing to sell Brown a typewriter, asks permission to place it in Brown's office so that Brown may try it for a time. While in Brown's office, and without any negligence on his part, the machine is stolen. Upon whom does the loss fall?

Answer   On Jones. Title to the machine does not pass to Brown until he evinces an. intention to buy and actually does purchase the typewriter. The mere fact that he permitted Jones to put the typewriter in his office indicates no such intention.

Question   Jones, in Baltimore, sells beer to Brown in Philadelphia, Jones to ship the beer to Brown at the latter's expense. Brown later refuses to pay, whereupon Jones sues Brown for the price of the beer. Brown's defense is that a sale of beer in Philadelphia without a license is illegal, and that Jones only has a Baltimore license. Is this a good defense?

Answer   No. Title to the beer passes in Baltimore, where the contract is made, and, since Jones has a Baltimore license, the sale is binding.

Question   Brown, in Baltimore, orders liquor from Jones, a dealer in Louisville, to be shipped C.O.D. On the way, but before delivery, the goods are destroyed. Upon whom does the loss fall?

Answer   On Jones, the dealer. In a sale where delivery is C.O.D. title does not pass until such delivery is actually made. Hence, the loss falls on the seller.

Question   Manning, in Baltimore, agrees to ship goods to Newman at Charleston, South Carolina, .F.O.B. (Free on Board) at

Norfolk, Virginia. Before the goods reach Norfolk they are destroyed. Upon whom does the loss fall?

Answer Loss falls on Manning in Baltimore. Under such an agreement as above, title does not pass until the goods reach Norfolk. Having been destroyed before reaching that city, the loss must be born by the seller, Manning.

Question Jones, in New York, consigns goods to himself at Kansas City. He forwards a bill of lading, indorsed in blank and with draft attached, to a bank, with directions that the bill be delivered only on payment of the draft. During transit, and before delivery of the bill of lading to Brown, the purchaser, the goods are damaged by flood; they are made practically worthless, and are not received by the connecting carrier in the flooded area. Upon who does the loss fall?

Answer On Jones. A. shipper who has the bill of lading made out to himself or his agent effects a retention of title in himself. A bill of lading is evidence of title; it may indicate that, although the seller made delivery to the carrier, he did not by that act appropriate the goods to the contract, but merely intended to reserve title or right of possession in himself. One way of retaining title is to send the bill of lading to some third person, usually a banker, with draft attached, which must be accepted, or, if a sight draft, paid, before the bill of lading can be secured. This reserves title, even though the bill of lading names the buyer as the consignee—the person to whom the goods are consigned.

Question Jones, owner of a lawnmower, leaves it with Brown to be sharpened. Brown sells it to Smith who does not know that Brown is not the actual owner, May Jones recover the lawn-mower from Smith?

Answer Yes. When Jones places the mower in Brown's possession, he may recover the machine even against Smith, an innocent purchaser, the theory being that Jones has never parted with legal possession of the machine. Since Brown never had legal ownership of the mower, he could not transfer ownership to Smith. Smith, however, has a right of action against Brown.

Question A merchant sells Collins some furniture on credit, which is duly delivered to him. Collins fails to pay for the goods as agreed. Can the merchant reclaim the goods?

Answer No. This is an outright sale, title passing to Collins. The merchants remedy is to sue and obtain judgment, then have it satisfied from such assets as he may discover in Collins' possession.

Question Jones buys an automobile from Brown, giving him his check in full for $500. Brown turns the car over to him. Later, when Brown attempts to cash the check, he finds it worthless. May Brown recover the car?

Answer Yes. One who obtains goods by giving a bad check, in what is intended by the seller to be a cash transaction in which no credit is given, may have the goods taken from him by the seller.

Question Suppose, in the above example, Jones sells the car to Smith, an innocent purchaser. May Brown reclaim the car from Smith?

Answer No. Title passed to Jones when he bought the ear. Upon the sale of the car to Smith he acquired title Brown's remedy would be to sue Jones and obtain a judgment against him.

Question Jones, owning an automobile, sells it to Brown. Brown however, allows Jones to remain in possession of the car for a few weeks. During this period, Jones sells the car to Thomas, an innocent purchaser. Who owns the car?

Answer Thomas. Brown, by allowing Jones to remain in possession; is precluded from denying Jones' authority to sell it to Thomas.

Question Jones sells Brown coffee, to be loaded by Jones on railway cars at Baltimore for shipment to Brown at Kansas City. The coffee is lost in transportation. Upon whom does the loss fall?

Answer Brown, since title passed in Baltimore. Brown must pay the agreed price and look to the carrier for his remedy, if any.

Question Peter sells vanilla to Jones, a candy manufacturer. Jones uses a considerable portion of vanilla as a test, when a fair. Test could be made by use of a few ounces. Jones then seeks to return the balance as being of poor quality. Can he do so

Answer No. Jones has a right to test, but his use in the present example 1s unreasonable and amounts to an acceptance.

Question Smith sells Peters a bill of goods on credit, to be shipped F.O.B. Chicago to San Francisco. Smith ships the goods via a railroad, the bill of lading being made out to Peters. While the goods are in transit Peters goes into bankruptcy. What can Smith do?

Answer	He may stop the goods in transit; if he does, the trustee in bankruptcy cannot claim them as part of Peters' estate. An unpaid seller, generally, has a lien against the goods for the agreed price, unless he agrees to sell on credit; where the buyer becomes insolvent, an unpaid seller may stop goods in transit, even after delivery to the carrier. He has a right also to resell the goods and, finally, a right to rescind the sale. The unpaid seller has these rights, even though title has passed If title has not passed, the goods are his and he may treat them as such upon non-performance by the buyer. He may even sue the buyer for damages occasioned by the breach.
Question	Jones and Company sends Brown and Company a sales memorandum in which it agrees to sell one thousand tons of scrap steel rails. The terms expressed are cash on presentation of draft attached to bill of lading. Brown and Company acknowledges the receipt of this memorandum, stating that the tails are to be of a certain pattern and that they are to come off a certain railway. Jones and Company replies that the rails are to come from a different railroad from the one named by Brown and Company. In the final letter of the exchange, Brown and Company answers that it is immaterial where the rails come from, but-insists that the rails be taken up from tracks, not be picked up from sidings along the road. Drafts, the letter concludes, will be honored when the cars arrive Is this a binding contract?
Answer	No. The letters show no agreement as to subject matter and terms of the sale. The agreement is too vague to be enforced.
Question	Jones and Company agrees to buy of Davis and Company, all the oyster shells made by the latter for the season beginning September 1st and ending May 1st, 19—which would amount to at least two hundred thousand bushels, and to pay on the first of each week for the shells delivered during the previous week. After seventy-five thousand bushels are delivered, Davis and Company notifies the Jones Company that the contract is at an end because of the Jones Company's failure to pay promptly each week. It appears that in October, Davis and Company had indorsed one of the weekly bills sent to Jones and Company, "Please send money for these bills promptly." A later bill contained

the indorsement, "Terms, cash every Monday." In a letter, Davis and Company insisted that the bills should be "paid promptly every week, as per agreement," and said that if they were not, Davis and Company would not allow Jones and Company to have any more shells. Jones and Company makes no objection to Davis and Company's construction of the contract. Does Davis and Company have a right to put an end to the contract?

Answer   Yes. The weekly payments agreed to be made to Davis and Company were of the essence of the contract. Since Jones and Company had often failed to make the payments on time, Davis and Company has a right to end the agreement.

Question   Jones, in Minneapolis, without authorization from Brown in Chicago, consigns to him a carload of flour for sale on commission, advising him of shipment and naming a price, but sending no bill of lading. While the flour is in transit, Jones sells it to Collins in Chicago, making out a bill of lading to him, and instructs the railroad company to change the markings on the flour and deliver it to Collins. Through failure of the company to carry out these instructions, the hour is delivered to Brown and sold by him. Collins, meanwhile, pays a draft on Brown for the amount of the flour and receives the bill of lading. Who is entitled to the flour?

Answer   Collins. The flour was sold to him, and he is entitled to recover the money received from the sale. Brown has no claim to the hour and Collins can recover against him.

Question   What is a "warranty" in the law of sales?

Answer   A warranty is an assertion, expressed or implied, by which the seller insures or guarantees that certain facts in connection with the sale are true, and upon which the buyer is induced to purchase the thing sold. Where there is a breach of warranty, the purchaser may return the goods within a reasonable time and recover the amount paid, or he may retain the goods and sue for breach of warranty.

Question   What implied warranties are there in a sale of goods?

Answer   In a sale, the seller warrants that he has a right to sell; in contracts to sell, he warrants that he will have a right to sell. The seller also warrants that the buyer will have and enjoy quiet possession of the thing sold against lawful claims existing at the time of sale. He also warrants that the goods are free from any incumbrance not known to the buyer.

Question Jones wants to sell his horse to Brown. The horse is at a place where the buyer may inspect him. Brown buys the horse but he shortly thereafter discovers that the horse is lame. He now wants his money back. Can he get it?

Answer No. Whether Brown inspects the horse or not, there is no implied warranty that the horse 18 sound. Even if the horse had a hidden disease, Jones would not be liable, unless he had knowledge of the disease.

Question Jones sells Brown an automobile, stating that it is a 19—model. Actually, it is a 19—car. Is Jones' statement a warranty?

Answer Yes. Here, Brown has a right to rely on Jones' statement that the car is a 19—model instead of a 19—model. This is not an expression of opinion but a fact, and if Brown is induced to buy the car on the strength of that statement, the statement becomes a warranty. Brown, therefore, may return the car within a reasonable time and recover the amount paid; or he may retain the car and sue for breach of warranty.

Question Jones sells Brown a certain mule for a reasonable price. The mule has a physical defect which cannot be ascertained upon a reasonable inspection. Jones knows the mule has the defect but he says nothing. Brown, discovering the defect later, sues Jones. Can he recover?

Answer Yes. Since Jones has knowledge of the defect, he is obliged to disclose it to Brown.

Question Jones offers to sell Brown a horse. When Brown inspects the animal, he notices that the horse has a slight limp. He mentions this to Jones who tells him that the limp is nothing serious. Jones tells Brown that he warrants, or guarantees, the horse to be sound in all respects, whereupon Brown buys the animal. The horse is, in fact, permanently lame. May Brown recover damages from Jones?

Answer Yes. Jones has warranted the soundness of the animal.

Question The seller of a horse agrees as part of the contract to deliver the animal's pedigree to the purchaser. After the sale is completed, the seller refuses to turn over the registration papers. Does the purchaser have a right of action?

Answer Yes. He may recover for a breach of warranty, since it is hardly likely that the sale would have taken place at the agreed price but for the fact that the animal has a pedigree.

Question   The seller of an automobile states that a certain car performs as well as any other car of the same make. On the strength of this statement the deal is closed. Shortly afterwards, the purchaser finds that his automobile by no means gives the performance that the car of the same make has been advertised as doing. What remedy has the buyer?

Answer   The above assertion is more than mere dealer's talk, and amounts in fact to a warranty. The purchaser, therefore, may either return the car and recover the amount paid, or retain it and sue for breach of warranty.

Question   Jones sells a used car to Brown, under a written contract which states that the car is sold "as is." Before signing, Brown expresses doubt about the battery. Jones says, "I will guarantee it for 5,000 more miles. If it gives out before that time, I will give you a new battery." Brown signs the contract and pays for the car. The next day the battery goes dead. Jones refuses to make good. Does Brown have a claim against Jones?

Answer   No. If a contract to sell, or a sale, is completely reduced to writing, as in the present case, alleged oral warranties cannot be introduced for the purpose of changing or adding to the written contract.

Question   Jones orders a ventilating fan from Brown to air a certain room. Brown agrees to furnish such a fan. Instead, he sends Jones a fan which does not adequately ventilate the room Jones had in mind. Must Jones accept the fan?

Answer   No Where goods are bought for a particular purpose, there is an implied warranty that the goods are fit for that purpose.

Question   Brown buys a quantity of blankets wrapped up in bales, the sale being made in a warehouse. Several pairs are pulled out, exhibited and found to be sound. Brown then buys twenty-five bales which he later discovers to be moth-eaten. What are Brown's rights?

Answer   In a sale by sample, there is an implied warranty that the goods will correspond with the sample. If the sale is by description as well as sample, the goods must correspond with the description. Hence, Brown can return the blankets and recover the money paid, or he may retain the blankets and sue for breach of warranty.

Question   A manufacturer sells Brown, a dealer, some goods, warranting that he has good title and that the goods are saleable. Brown resells the goods to a customer who finds that they are defective. May the customer sue the manufacturer on the latter's warranty to Brown?

Answer   No. A warranty by a seller to a buyer is a contract between the two, the rights to which do not pass to one who buys from the original purchaser.

Question   Jones sells Brown a quantity of tobacco, delivering a bill which describes it as follows; "24 kegs of tobacco, branded Parkin, at 4 months, weighing etc., at $13^{1/2}$ cents." Jones sells the tobacco on commission. The tobacco is branded as stated in the bill of parcels and is not examined by either party prior to, or at the time of, the sale. The price agreed is a full price for merchantable commodity. When Brown examines the tobacco after the sale he finds part of it unsound. Does Brown have a claim against Jones?

Answer   No. There was no implied warranty of quality in this contract, since nothing was stipulated as to the quality of the tobacco. Jones' terms were complied with by the delivery of the tobacco in conformance with the bill of parcels.

Question   You buy a leaf of bread at a, grocery store, naming the brand, which is handed to you in the original wrapper. You later find a nail concealed in the bread which causes injury to one of your teeth. May you sue the grocery store or must you proceed against the bread manufacturer?

Answer   You may sue the grocer from whom you bought the bread. When the grocer sold the bread, he impliedly warranted or guaranteed its quality. The concealment of a foreign substance is a breach of that warranty. The grocer, for his part, may recoup himself against loss by proceeding against the bread maker.

Question   Jones sells goods to Brown, under an agreement that Brown may return the goods at any time within thirty days if he finds them unsatisfactory. While the goods are in Brown's possession, they are destroyed by fire without fault on Brown's part. Who must bear the loss?

Answer   Brown. Under such an agreement, the goods belong to Brown. Where one sells merchandise "on sale or return," the sale takes place immediately; title passes at once, subject to the condition that the buyer may return the goods and revest the title within the stipulated period. Had the goods not been destroyed, Brown could have returned them at any time within the thirty days. Until such return within thirty days. the goods are subject to seizure by Brown's creditors. Risk of loss is on Brown at all times from the moment he receives the goods until he makes the return, or an offer of return.

Question A contract for the sale of a gasoline engine provides that "if the engine does not do our work we are to ship it elsewhere after giving it a trial." The buyer of the engine fails to return it within the time limited by the contract. A day or two after the time limit expires, the engine explodes and is totally destroyed-without any negligence on the part of the buyer, and before he had tested it. Upon whom does the loss fall?

Answer The buyer. This is an absolute sale with an option on the part of the buyer to cancel the sale and return the engine. Title, therefore, passes immediately to the buyer; he is liable for the contract price.

Question On August 23, 19—, a manufacturer agrees to build certain machines to turn out specified work and to install them in the mill of the buyer within six months, it being agreed that the machines are "to be to the full satisfaction of the buyer as to quality, life, and durability before payment for them will be required." The time is extended to April 22, 19—when the buyer rejects all the machines. The manufacturer is unable to get his money, even though the buyer has made some use of the machines. Can the manufacturer recover the contract price?

Answer No—since, under the contract, the machines were to be to the full satisfaction of the buyer. Of course, in rejecting them the buyer must act in good faith and be honestly dissatisfied. The manufacturer can only recover his machines. Since there was never a contract-the condition not having been fulfilled-he cannot sue for the purchase price of the machines.

Question Smith, by correspondence, buys a steam engine, pump, etc., on condition that the same be set up on his premises by the seller, for a thirty-day trial period. If the machinery is found unsatisfactory, it is to be made good or moved at the expense of the seller. The machinery is set up and run for six months, without any objections. Then Smith assigns the machinery, with the premises, to his landlord. The seller seeks to recover the purchase price of the machinery. May he do so?

Answer Yes. Even if Smith has a continuing option to reject the machinery as not being satisfactory, the option is ended and the sale becomes absolute when he assigns the property tor third person.

Question What is a "conditional sale agreement"?

Answer Such an agreement is one by which goods are sold and title reserved by the seller until a certain condition is performed by the buyer, such as paying the price, for example. Upon breach of the condition, the seller may either retake the goods or sue to recover their value.

Question Mrs. Brown buys a refrigerator at a furniture store. She signs a conditional sale agreement in which it is agreed that she is to pay $15 monthly until the purchase price is paid in full. The refrigerator is delivered, Mrs. Brown makes three payments, then cannot continue. What can the store do?

Answer Under such a conditional sale agreement, the store may retake the refrigerator and retain the payments already made. Theoretically, the store may even resell the refrigerator at a loss, if necessary, and sue Mrs. Brown for the difference between the original purchase price and the amount it was forced to accept on the resale.

Question Jones buys an automobile under a conditional sale agreement whereby he gives $100 as deposit, agreeing to pay the balance in equal monthly installments until the full purchase price is paid. While in Jones' possession and without any negligence on his part, the car is completely destroyed by fire. Is Jones liable for the full purchase price of the car?

Answer Yes. Under a conditional sale agreement, the automobile company may sue Jones and recover judgment against him or the unpaid balance.

Question Brown agrees with Jones that the latter may send him a washing machine "on trial" for sixty days. While in Brown's possession the machine is damaged. Upon whom does the loss fall?

Answer On Jones. Under such an agreement Brown has not purchased the machine and title does not pass to him until the sixty days have expired. If Brown does not return the goods within sixty days, title will pass to him; he cannot thereafter return the machine. During the sixty days, unless Brown has, before the end of the period, signified his acceptance, the risk of loss is on Jones—unless the loss occurs by Brown's negligence. Moreover, the creditors of Jones could seize the machine, since Brown has no right in it against Jones' creditors, as he is under no contract to buy it.

Question Jones sells a motorcycle to Brown, payment to be made in six monthly installments. Brown is to have possession at once, but title is not to pass until all payments are made. The contract also provides that, in case of default by Brown, Jones might retake the motorcycle at any time. Brown defaults after the second payment and Jones retakes the motorcycle. Jones sues Brown for the unpaid balance due. Can he recover?

Answer No. Courts frequently hold that a seller who has retaken possession, under a conditional sale agreement, cannot thereafter sue for the price. Upon breach by the buyer, the seller may recover either the goods or the price, but not both.

Question George buys a piano on a conditional sale agreement. After making a few payments, he sells it to his friend Harry, at a loss, for cash. George makes no further payments on the piano. What can the piano company do about it?

Answer It can retake the piano from Harry. Harry's remedy, in turn, is a suit against George.

Advisory 5

INSURANCE

Insurance is a method by which man guards himself against the hazards of life.

More than a hundred years ago, a committee of the British House of Commons, investigating insurance, laid down the principle that "whenever there is a contingency, the cheapest way of providing against it is by uniting with others, so that each man may subject himself to a small deprivation, in order that no man may be subjected to a great loss."

This principle, first enunciated in 1825, has since proved its soundness and wisdom. Insurance today is a big business, represented by nearly one hundred and thirty million policies of all kinds, and some $124,000,000,000 of insurance in force.

Unfortunately, few of us ever take the time and trouble to read our policies. For the most part, we accept without question what our agent tells us about them, never doubting his interpretation of the policy or his authority to act for and on behalf of his company. Such implicit faith, though touching, often gives rise to serious difficulties, including law suits.

A policy, it must be remembered, is a contract containing the terms agreed upon by the company and policyholder; it is interpreted and governed by the same principles controlling other contracts.

Question   What is insurance?

Answer   It is an agreement by which one party, for a consideration, usually money, promises to pay a certain sum upon the destruction or injury of something in which the other party has an interest. The insurer is sometimes called the underwriter. The insured is also called the assured.

Question   What is meant by a premium?

Answer   It is the agreed consideration paid by the insured to the insurer, usually money.

Question   What is a policy?

Answer   It is the written contract embodying the terms agreed upon between the parties. It is usually issued upon the application of the insured in writing.

Question   What is meant by the "loss"?

Answer   It is the happening of the event insured against, and the consequent damage to the subject matter.

Question   What is life insurance?

Answer   This is a contract by which the insurer, in consideration of a certain premium, undertakes to pay the person for whose benefit the insurance is made a stipulated sum upon the death of the insured.

Question   What is meant by the term "double indemnity," as contained in a life insurance policy?

Answer   This provision stipulates that, in the event the assured meets with an accidental death While a passenger on a common carrier such as a train, street car, taxicab, steamer, airplane, etc., the company will pay double the face value of the policy. Thus, where an individual is accidentally killed while a passenger on a train, and has a $ 5,000 life policy containing a "double indemnity" clause, his beneficiary or estate will receive $10,000.

Question   What is endowment insurance?

Answer   It is an agreement by which the insurer, for a consideration, promises to pay a specific sum of money at a time stated, or at the insured's death, if it occurs earlier than the date fixed for payment.

Question   What is accident insurance?

Answer   This provides for specified payments in case of an accident resulting in bodily injury or death.

Question   What is casualty insurance?

Answer   It is a contract which provides for payments in case of loss or damage to property, caused by accident. For example, the loss of horses or cattle, theft of valuables, breakage of plate glass, etc.

Question   What is fire insurance?

Answer   It is a contract by which the insurer, in consideration of a stipulated premium, undertakes to compensate the insured. against all loss or damage sustained to a certain amount in the property mentioned in the policy by fire, during the time agreed upon.

Question What is marine insurance?

Answer This is a contract of indemnity by which the insurer, for an agreed premium, undertakes to indemnify or compensate the insured to the extent of the amount insured against such perils of the sea as are enumerated in the policy.

Question What is employer's liability insurance?

Answer It is a contract by which the insurer agrees to reimburse an employer for any loss due to his liability for damages to an employee injured in his service.

Question What is fidelity insurance?

Answer It is a contract Which protects the insured against loss due to the default or dishonesty of an employee.

Question What is assessment insurance?

Answer Such insurance provides that money to pay a death loss or claim be collected by an assessment made upon those members who survive the policy holder, the insurance upon whose life is paid. In standard insurance companies, the amount of the premium is definitely fixed. In an assessment insurance policy, the right is usually reserved to increase or lower the rates of assessment or premium. Hence, under an assessment policy, the premium is not definitely fixed and the members may be called upon to pay a much larger premium or assessment than they had anticipated.

Question What is credit insurance?

Answer This is a policy by which the insured is compensated against loss by the failure of his customers to pay for goods sold to them. In such policies, the insured is frequently called the "indemnified" and is so referred to in the policy.

Question What is industrial insurance?

Answer This is a life insurance policy for a small or limited amount in consideration of a premium, payable in small installments and collectible weekly or at some other short, periodic interval. It includes both adult and child insurance and amounts, in fact, to burial insurance.

Question What is strike insurance?

Answer This type of policy provides that the insurer shall, for a consideration, indemnify and guarantee individuals or business firms against damage or loss due to, or by reason of strike.

Question What is title insurance?

Answer This contract indemnifies the owner or mortgagee of real estate from loss by reason of defective titles, liens or incumbrances.

Question What is meant by insurable interest?

Answer This is a legally recognized interest in the person or thing insured which the one taking the insurance policy must have. Generally, the reasonable expectation of benefit or advantage from the continued life of another creates an insurable interest in such life. The same applies to an interest in property.

Question Tom would like to take out a policy of insurance on his friend's house. He has no interest in it. Will he be issued a policy?

Answer No. He lacks an "insurable interest" in his friend's property. The law frowns upon and forbids such insurance, viewing the transaction in the nature of a gambling wager which might lead to the property's destruction.

Question Mary takes out a policy on her own life, making her lover the beneficiary. She pays the first three premiums, her lover the remainder. After Mary's death, the boyfriend demands payment on the policy from the company. The company refuses. Who is right?

Answer The company. The boyfriend has no "insurable interest" in Mary's death.

Question Aunt Ada has reared Esther, her thirteen-year-old niece, in the expectation that the child would be a help in the aunt's old age. A $10,000 policy is taken out by Aunt Ada on Esther's life. A year later, the niece dies and her aunt seeks to recover on the policy Can she do so?

Answer Yes. Mere relationship alone is insufficient to create an "insurable interest," except on the case of husband and wife, but in the above example there is more than mere relationship. There is, in addition, the expectation of benefit or support to be derived from the continuance of the life of the insured; there is also a reasonable chance that the services will be rendered, even though Esther never has the opportunity to support Aunt Ada.

Question Jim, a friend, borrows $5,000 from you. To protect your interest, you insure his life for $7,500, making yourself the beneficiary and paying the first premium. Later, Jim pays the debt in full. You continue to pay all premiums on the policy until Jim's death. May you recover on the policy?

Answer   Yes. In most states, however, you may retain only the amount of premiums you paid on the policy, the balance going to Jim's estate. As a creditor, you have an "insurable interest" in Jim; also, the amount of insurance is reasonable when compared to the risk. But when the debt is paid the "insurable interest" is lost, and you will be able to retain only the premiums you have paid.

Question   A daughter insures her father's life—without his knowledge or consent. After the father's death, the daughter seeks to recover the face value of the policy. May she?

Answer   No. Strictly speaking, it is necessary for the beneficiary to give his consent before an insurance contract becomes binding. Upon the death of the father, all that the daughter can recover is the money she paid in as premiums.

Question   What is the difference between a warranty and a representation in insurance law?

Answer   A warranty is an essential part of the contract, agreed by both parties to be essential. A representation is but a collateral inducement. A warranty is always written on the face of the policy. A representation need not be written in the policy and may be merely an oral statement. A warranty is conclusively presumed to be material, so that upon its breach the company can cancel the policy. The importance of a representation, on the other hand, must be proved by the insurance company before it can avoid the policy. Finally, a warranty must be strictly complied with; a representation need only be substantially complied with.

Question   In an application for insurance on his life Brown is asked: "Have you, at any time, had any disease of the heart? To this he answers: "No." The application refers to all answers as "warranties." A photostatic copy of the application is pasted on the policy and expressly incorporated in it. In the policy, however, all answers are called representations. Brown passes the physical examination and a policy is issued to him, A year later, he dies of heart disease. The company refused to pay because it learns, after his death, that Brown had long been affected with a heart disease, difficult to detect. His family doctor had discovered the ailment several years he fore, but had never told Brown for fear it would more seriously impair his health. The ailment, however, did not interfere with Brown's work. May the beneficiary recover on the policy?

Answer   Yes. The controlling question here is whether Brown's statement is a warranty. A warranty is a stipulation, material to the risk, on the exact truth and fulfillment of which depends the insurance company's obligation to pay. With the exception of marine insurance, a warranty must be a term of the policy, Or, if in a separate paper, the paper must be permanently attached to and made an integral part of the policy. If the paper is not physically attached to the policy, there must be an express provision in the policy incorporating the statement. Any clause expressly called a warranty is usually interpreted as such, but this is not the invariable rule. Brown's answer is called a warranty, is physically part of the policy, incorporated by express statement, and is material to the risk. This makes the answer, at first blush, a warranty. It will then have to be literally correct for the policy will be avoided, since an unqualified statement as to health, warranted to be true, usually nullifies the policy if, in fact, it is false. In warranties, the good faith of the applicant is immaterial. But is Brown's answer a warranty? Although the application calls it one, the policy itself refers to it as a representation. This creates an ambiguity Which is resolved against the company. Hence, Brown's answer is a representation and will not be strictly construed against him. The insurance company, therefore, must prove that the fact is material and the presentation false. Brown's statement is only an honest expression of his opinion. It is not fraudulent. His heart ailment did not interfere with his work and, at the time of the application, was not present in an advanced stage. In short, Brown answered the question in good faith; his beneficiary could recover.

Question In an application for a fire insurance policy Brown, owner of a factory, in answer to the question, "Who sleeps in the store?" wrote, "Watchman on premises at night." A few days later, his factory burns down. The insurance company has evidence that Brown did not employ a watchman the night of the fire. Can the insurance company refuse payment?

Answer   No. This statement, made a warranty by the policy, refers only to the time when the contract was made and was not a warranty that a watchman would be kept on the premises continuously.

Question   Prior to taking out a life insurance policy, Jones, a heavy drinker, consulted two physicians about his ulcerated stomach. In his application for insurance he states that he has not consulted a physician within five years from the date of the application, and that he uses liquor sparingly. Upon Jones' death, his wife, the beneficiary, attempts to recover on the policy. Will she succeed?

Answer   No. A false representation as to health will not necessarily bar recovery on a policy. The representation, to bar recovery, must be material to the risk. In this case, however, the false statement is material, for if Jones' ulcers had been known to the company, the company would probably have turned down the application, especially since the falsity of the statement was coupled with the additional fact of Jones' drinking.

Question   In his application for life insurance, Smith fails to mention that he has a perforated eardrum. A few years after the policy goes into effect, Smith dies of a heart ailment. The insurance company refuses to pay the face amount of the policy to the beneficiary. Is it justified in so doing?

Answer   No. In this case, there is no connection between the perforated ear drum and the fatal heart disease. Hence, the company is bound to pay.

Question   In his application for life insurance, Garfield states that he has suffered no ill health for five years and that he has not consulted a physician for ten years. Actually, a physician treated him twice for indigestion shortly before Garfield made out the application. After the first premium is paid, Garfield dies from a heart attack. The company refuses payment. What is the result?

Answer   In a similar case, the court decided that the insurance company would have to pay. The court held that Garfield's failure to mention that he had indigestion several weeks before making out the application and had received treatment by a physician was not sufficient bad faith to justify the company's refusal to pay.

Question   An insurance agent obtains from Mrs. Holmes an application for insurance upon the life of her husband. The application is signed in blank (without the relevant information being filled in). The agent fills in the application, first making inquiries of Mr. Holmes who answers correctly the questions asked by the agent. However, the agent inserts incorrect statements in the policy. The application is sent to the insurer who issues a policy thereon, without further inquiry. After the death of Mr. Holmes, the insurer refuses payment on the ground that the agent inserted in the application several false material answers to questions asked Mr. Holmes. The insurer contends that if the agent had inserted the correct answers given by Mr. Holmes, the company would never have accepted the risk. Does the company have to make good on the policy?

Answer   Yes. The agent is acting for the insurer and not for Mr. Holmes, the insurance company being charged with knowledge acquired by the agent. Hence, the company will be bound. Stated another way, the answers are those of the agent, not Mr. Holmes, and the insurer will be bound by the act of its agent.

Question   In filling out an application for life insurance, Brown, on the advice of the agent, omits the fact that he is a member of the U. S. Naval Reserve and therefore liable to naval service. Instead, he describes himself as a fisherman. His connection with the Naval Reserve is communicated by the agent to the district manager of the company who fails to disclose the fact to the home office. The policy is issued by the company. While in the Naval Reserve, Brown is lost at sea. The insurer refuses to pay on the policy. Must it do so?

Answer   Yes. The insurer is liable, the company being charged with the knowledge of its district manager. When the district manager accepted the premium with knowledge of the concealment, the insurer waived its defense.

Question   Brown, a farmer, orally applies for hail insurance on a certain described crop of grain. He fails to mention that there is a chattel mortgage on the crop, and the insurer's agent does not make any inquiry in that respect. The policy is issued and accepted by Brown who does not read it. The policy, however, contains a clause making it void if there is a chattel mortgage on the crop of grain. Farmer Brown pays the premium and lays the policy, still unread, in his bureau drawer in the belief that his interest in the crop is protected. After the crop is destroyed by hail, Brown learns for the first time that he is actually not protected. The insurer refuses to pay, on the ground that Brown failed to disclose the chattel mortgage. Can the assured recover?

Answer   Yes—in most states, on the theory that the farmer was misled into thinking that he had an adequate policy and that the agent was neglectful in making proper inquiry into the matter. Under the above facts, the insurer is probably prevented or "estopped" from denying the soundness of the policy he sold.

Question A fire insurance policy contains a clause that the company will not be liable until the premium is actually paid in full. A later condition provides that the insured should be allowed a certain time to pay the premium but that if the insured does not pay the premium within that time, the policy is to be null and void. The property is destroyed before the premium is paid, as well as before the expiration of the time limited for its payment. Can the insured recover on the policy?

Answer Since the fire occurred before the payment of the premium the risk never attached and the company is not liable.

Question An insurance policy on a building contains a stipulation that if the building is used to carry on the trade of a carpenter, etc. the policy is to be void so long as any portion of the premises are so used. While the policy is in force, a box factory is established on the premises but work there is temporarily suspended for some months before the building is destroyed by fire. After the fire, the assured seeks to recover on the loss. May he?

Answer Yes. The fact that the building was used temporarily for carpenter work merely suspends the policy for that period of time. When the box factory suspended operations, the policy again went into effect.

Question A fire insurance policy provides that it shall become void if the building described therein becomes vacant or unoccupied and remains so for ten days. The assured, occupant of the house, moves on June 18th to another city and does not return until July 6th. The house is destroyed by fire the day before her return what is on July 5th. Although the furniture had been removed, the husband occasionally visited the former home. May the assured recover on her policy?

Answer No. The policy is cancelled under the clause against vacancy; that the husband occasionally visited the premises does not alter the fact that, for legal purposes, the house was vacant for more than ten days.

Question A fire insurance policy provides that the insured is not to keep on the assured premises any articles deemed hazardous, except as provided in the policy or thereafter agreed to by the company. This agreement is later changed by the following indorsement on the policy: "Permission given to keep one barrel of benzine in tin cans for use on the premises." A barrel of benzine is brought in; it is being emptied into a large tin can when it explodes, setting fire to and destroying the building. May the insured recover?

Answer   Yes. There is a substantial compliance with the terms of the indorsement in keeping the benzine in one tin can.

Question   A fire insurance policy provides that it shall be void if any change takes place in the interest, title or possession of the property, whether by legal process or by a voluntary act of the insured. A few days before the building is destroyed by fire, the assured enters into a contract of sale for the building, but fails to notify the company. After the fire, the assured seeks to recover on the policy. May he?

Answer   No. Entering into a contract of sale is a breach of the condition imposed by the company; the assured cannot recover on the loss.

Question   Brown's fire insurance policy on his toy shop insures "fancy goods, toys and other articles in his line of business." A clause written with pen and ink in the body of the policy grants "permission to keep fireworks on hand." Under a printed clause, however, the insurance is avoided if the insured "keeps" certain hazardous articles, including fireworks. Toy shops usually have fireworks in stock, and there are fireworks worth about $35 on Brown's shelves for several months. No fireworks are on hand at the time of the fire, May Brown recover on the policy when his toy shop burns down?

Answer   Yes. Where a written provision conflicts with the printed clause, the written provision governs. Written provisions are for the particular instance. Printed clauses are for general use. Most courts would probably find that the parties intended to allow the keeping of fireworks, especially since they had nothing to do with the loss.

Question   Brown, deeply in debt, insures his life for $35,000, making his wife the beneficiary. At the time he takes out the insurance, he fully intends to mature the policy by committing suicide in order to make provision for his wife.

The policy is expressly made "incontestable" after it has been in force two years from the date of issue. It stipulates that the insurance is to take effect only on delivery of the policy and payment of the first premium. By another clause the policy is avoided "if the insured shall commit suicide within two years from the date hereof." The policy is dated January 12, 19—. It is delivered and the first premium paid on January 30th, of the same year. On January 20, 19—, two years later, Brown kills himself. The insurance company notifies the beneficiary on the twenty-fifth of the same month that it will not pay because of the suicide. May the wife recover on the policy?

Answer   Yes. The "suicide" clause makes the policy void if the insured commits suicide within two years from the "date hereof" which means the date of the policy, January 12th. The suicide took place January 20th, more than two years after the "date hereof"; therefore, the suicide clause does not bar recovery.

Question   Brown takes out fire insurance on his farm dwelling house with one insurance company and insurance on his furniture with another company. The policy on the house provides that "this entire policy shall be void if the insured building be or become vacant or unoccupied and so remain for ten days." The policy on the furniture provides that "The insurance company shall not be liable for a loss to the insured property by lightning." The application for each policy, signed by Brown, contains a clause providing that "No agent shall have power to waive any provision in the policy nor shall any waiver be valid unless in writing, indorsed on the policy at the home office by the President, Vice President or Secretary." Brown tells Smith, the general agent of the fire insurance company which wrote the insurance on the house, that he will close the farmhouse the following month and move into the city for the winter. Smith gives his consent, delivering the policy to Brown, but without any indorsement. A month later, Brown closes his farmhouse and takes up residence in town. Later, the farmhouse is struck by lightning; fire springs up and the house and furniture are totally destroyed. No indorsement had been made on the furniture policy, either. On learning of the loss, the insurance company which covered the furniture writes Brown, advising that his claim will be considered at a meeting of the Board of Directors of the company. Both insurance companies, however, deny liability. Can Brown recover against either or both companies?

Answer   He can recover against neither. He cannot recover on the policy on the house, since Brown violated the clause forbidding vacancy. The "vacancy" clause is a condition, a breach of which gives the insurance company the option to cancel. It is true that Smith, a general agent, had all the powers of his company with respect to making the contract. He even had the power to waive the requirement of an indorsement and did so by delivering the policy with knowledge of the breach. However, a general agent's oral promise, made before or at the time the policy is written, to waive a future breach of a condition in the policy, is not binding on the company, such oral evidence being inadmissible to contradict the policy. Brown could not recover on his furniture policy, since the loss by lightning was an "excepted" risk—that is, one not covered by the terms of the policy.

Question   Brown informs an insurance company agent that he wishes to apply for life insurance as he is about to enter military service. He knows this is contrary to a condition in the proposed policy. The agent, however, tells Brown that the company will not enforce the condition. Thereupon, Brown makes application and receives a policy containing a clause that the policy shall become void if Brown engages in military. service without the consent of the company indorsed on the policy. Brown, without such indorsed consent, is drafted into the army and is killed in action. His beneficiary seeks to recover on the policy. Can he?

Answer   No. The agent's verbal agreement cannot be introduced to contradict the policy. Even if the agent's statement had been reduced to writing, it could not contradict the policy, since the company's written indorsement was not obtained.

Question   Brown obtains insurance on his printing office and bookbindery. The policy contains a printed condition relieving the insurer for any loss or damage by lire caused by camphene or other inflammable liquids. In the description of the property insured is found the clause, "privileged for printing office, bindery, etc." The property is destroyed by a tire caused by the ignition of camphene, kept by Brown for the purpose of cleaning the presses. Is the insurer liable under the policy?

Answer   Yes. A general usage may be shown as existing among printers to keep camphene in their shops, and that such usage is necessary in the conduct of the business.

Question   Dick files an application for a $5,000 policy on his life, payable to his wife. He pays his premium, the receipt for it reading as follows; "The insurance is not to be in force until the application is approved, accepted, and the policy delivered by the company to the applicant while in good health." Dick passes the physical examination, but the company decides,
because of his past habit of drinking, to write the insurance for $2,500 only. A policy in that amount is mailed to the insurance agent, with instructions to deliver it to Dick. The agent tells Dick by telephone that his policy arrived that morning. That same afternoon, Dick is killed in an automobile accident. May Dick's widow collect on the policy?

Answer   Yes, $5,000. An oral contract of life insurance is legal, unless a state law requires it to be in writing. Dick was in good health when the policy was mailed to the agent. He also had a right to believe that the policy was written in accordance with his application. Otherwise, being in good health, he could have insured with another company. The first premium had been paid, and when the agent informed Dick that his policy had arrived the company became bound.

Question   While chopping wood, a piece of it flies up in Brown's face, causing an abrasion of the skin. Infection sets in, resulting in blood poisoning and death. Two years before, Brown had suffered from a severe attack of blood poisoning. He had recovered but was more susceptible to infection than the average person. May Brown's beneficiary recover on his accident insurance policy, insuring against the results of bodily injuries caused directly by violent and accidental means?

Answer   Yes. Since Brown did not intend or expect to get blood poisoning when he chopped the wood, the result of his act is accidental. The fact that Brown's system was weakened by the previous attack of blood poisoning is immaterial, since this was not an active factor. In general, accident policies are construed against the company and in favor of the insured.

Question   Brown takes out an accident policy. Subsequently, he dies

	from an infection caused by the extraction of a tooth. Is the insurer liable?
Answer	Yes. Though the extraction of the tooth is intended, and hence not accidental, the result is unexpected; the company, therefore, would be liable.
Question	Brown takes out an accident policy. Undertaking to swim, against a swift current, Brown so overexerts himself as to cause a hemorrhage, from which he dies. Is the insurer liable?
Answer	No. Here, the acts which led to Brown's death could normally be expected, even though the resulting injury was unexpected.
Question	Brown, heated from playing a strenuous game of tennis, takes (as he frequently does under similar conditions) a cold bath which unexpectedly causes a heart attack, disabling him for several months. He seeks to recover under his accident policy. Can he do so?
Answer	No. Since Brown took the cold bath voluntarily to cool off, without slipping or falling, with the water at the intended temperature, the unusual result was not caused by accidental means within the terms of his policy.
Question	Brown, suffering from a cold, takes a fatal overdose of some medicine and dies. Is the insurer liable under an accident policy?
Answer	Yes. The overdose was accidental, since Brown merely intended to take a safe quantity of medicine.
Question	Brown places an unclean hand upon a boil which becomes infected and from which he dies. Is the insurer liable under an accident policy?
Answer	No. There is nothing accidental about this death. If Brown did not, in fact, foresee infection, he should have done so.
Question	Nurse Jones has an accident policy. She dies from inhaling streptococcic germs while attending a patient ill from blood poisoning. Would the insurer be liable?
Answer	Yes.
Question	While wearing a new shoe, Brown's toe becomes bruised; blood poisoning sets in from which Brown dies. Is the insurer liable under an accident policy?
Answer	Yes. If the circumstances are such as to make the accident, and not the disease, the proximate cause of the death, the insurer will be liable, as for death due to accidental means. In this case, the accident was due to Brown's rubbing his

toe in the new shoe, even though he actually died from blood poisoning, a disease.

Question Brown's accident policy contains a clause relieving the insurer from liability for injury by taking poison. Brown drinks carbolic acid, thinking it to be peppermint, and dies from the poisoning. Would the insurer be liable?

Answer Yes. Generally, such clauses exempt the insurer where the insured takes poison intentionally, not when he takes it mistakenly.

Question Brown's policy contains a clause exempting the insurer where the insured's injuries are, due to his voluntary and unnecessary exposure to injury. While painting a house, Brown falls off the scaffold, breaking his leg. The insurance company refuses to pay on the ground that, in voluntarily exposing himself to injury, Brown violated his policy. Is the insurer liable?

Answer Yes—since the exposure, though voluntary, was necessary in Brown's business.

Question Smith's accident policy contains a clause relieving the insurer from liability for death while engaged in military service. Smith is drafted into the army. While riding in his jeep from one sawmill to another, supervising construction, Smith's vehicle skids and he is killed. Is the insurer liable?

Answer Yes. Such clauses as the one described above limit the company's responsibility only when the injury results from some cause peculiar to the military service. It does not apply where the injury, as in the present case, is one common to civilian life as well.

Question An insurance company was incorporated on July 24th. On August 7th, Smith applies for coverage on his house, the application being subject to the approval of the Board of Directors. The application is handed to one of the directors on August 9th, and on August 22nd he delivers it to the secretary of the company. A quorum not being present at the time, no business is transacted. A special meeting of the Board of Directors is held on August 19th, but the application is not considered. On August 30th, the house is destroyed by fire. At the first regular meeting of the Executive Committee, held on September 25th, the application is rejected and this action is approved by the Board. Brown seeks to recover on his policy. Can he?

Answer No. In a similar case the court ruled that the company had not failed to act on the application within a reasonable time and its conduct was not calculated to mislead Smith.

Question An insurance broker is authorized to take applications and write policies. Blank forms for the purpose are supplied him by the four or five fire companies he represents. You telephone the broker, asking him to insure your house for three years for $2,000. The broker tells you that you are covered, later making a notation to that effect on his file card. The following day, your house burns down before the broker sends you the policy. Are you covered?

Answer Yes, upon your offer to pay the premium. Insurance contracts, to be binding, need not be in writing. Both you and the broker have agreed on the name of the insured, the property, the amount of insurance and the duration of the cover age. Although nothing is said about the premium, the law presumes the customary rate is intended. And, though the premium is not paid before the fire occurs, the law will assume that credit was extended by the broker.

Question You make a binding contract for the purchase of a house. After the contract is completed, but before the deed is turned over to you, the house is destroyed by tire. The seller is still in possession of the house and had previously taken out a policy of fire insurance on it. Both the seller of the house and you, as the buyer, claim the insurance money. Who is entitled to it?

Answer The seller. The contract of insurance is purely personal between the company and the seller of the house, and you, as buyer, have no rights in it.

Question Smith, an insurance agent, tenders to Brown a life policy containing a provision that it shall not take effect until actually delivered to the insured while he is in good health and the first premium is paid in cash. Brown explains that he does not have any ready money, offering to give his note, at six months, for the premium. The agent accepts the note and delivers the policy. Brown dies within the six months. Must the insurance company pay?

Answer Yes. Assuming that he has the requisite authority, the agent can remove the condition requiring prepayment of the first premium in cash. The insurance company, by its agent's duly authorized act, "waives" the condition and will be bound to pay on the policy.

Question Brown's policy contains an anti-military service clause.

Enlisting in the army, Brown serves without injury and is discharged. He informs the agent of these facts, offering to pay the next accruing premium. The agent accepts it, saying that, while the policy had been forfeited, the company would waive the forfeiture. A few days after the premium is accepted, Brown dies and the insurance company now refuses to pay on the policy. Can it be compelled to do so?

Answer Yes. In accepting the premium, the agent waived the forfeiture and the insurance company will be bound.

Question Smith's fire policy contains a provision that no action shall be brought on it unless satisfactory proofs of loss are, furnished within sixty days after the fire. Immediately after a fire, Smith applies for forms on which to make his proofs of loss. He is told by the insurance company that such proofs are unnecessary, since liability under the policy is denied because of Smith's breach of the condition against other insurance. A few weeks after the sixty-day period is up, Smith through his lawyer, seeks to recover on the policy. The company now defends, on the ground that proofs of loss were not tiled as required within the sixty days, Is such a defense good?

Answer No. When an insurer denies all liability under the contract, the courts generally hold that all conditions still to be performed by the insured are waived.

Question Brown's life insurance policy contains a provision excepting from the risks covered by the contract death or injury suffered while in military service. Brown is killed while engaged in battle, but the sympathetic insurance company, with full knowledge of the facts, agrees to waive the exception. Later; the company changes its mind and refuses to pay the beneficiary. Can it be compelled to do so?

Answer No. The original contract does not cover such a loss. The promise of the company to pay is unenforceable, unless there is a legal consideration to support the new promise. Since
there was no such consideration in this case, the company would not be bound.

Question Brown, holder of a life policy, fails to pay his premium, due on June 15th. On June 25th, he pays the premium to the agent who has knowledge of all the facts. On June 30th, Brown dies and the insurance company refuses payment on

	the policy. Is it justified in doing so?
Answer	No. The acceptance of an overdue premium by an agent having authority to do so shows an intention to continue the policy in full force.
Question	A provision on Jackson's fire insurance policy declares that the policy will be null and void should the insured procure other insurance without the consent of the company, to he noted on the policy. Without such consent, Jackson procures other insurance, notifying the fire insurance company which makes no response to the notice. Two months later, a fire occurs and the insurer refuses to pay on the policy. Is it correct in doing so?
Answer	No. When the company first received notice, it had a right to take advantage of the provisions of its policy. When it remained silent for two months after notice was given it, Jackson was deprived of any opportunity to protect himself by getting still other insurance. The insurance company, by its silence, waived its rights to avoid the policy.
Question	Brown's fire insurance policy contains a provision that "agents of the company are not authorized to make, alter or abrogate contracts or waive forfeitures." The policy also provides that a failure to pay any premium or note at maturity renders the policy null and void. The evidence shows that the company did, in fact, allow its agents to extend the time for the payment of premium notes, despite the restriction mentioned in the policy. Brown, after the maturity of a premium note, secures an extension of time from the agent and dies before the expiration of the extended time. The insurer refuses payment on the policy. Can it be compelled to pay?
Answer	Yes. Brown's beneficiary can, through counsel, introduce evidence tending to prove that the agent permitted an extension of time in which to pay the note, and that it was customary for the company to waive its policy provisions with reference to the payment of premiums
Question	Smith takes out a life policy, making his wife unconditionally the beneficiary. After a quarrel, Smith and his wife live separate and apart. Smith refuses to pay the premiums. How may the wife protect her interests in the policy?
Answer	By continuing to pay the premiums on her husband's policy. Of course, where the policy reserves the right on the part of the insured to change the beneficiary, Smith can defeat

his wife's interest by changing the beneficiary.

Question Brown takes out a life insurance policy, designating his wife, Helen, as beneficiary. Subsequently, Brown divorces Helen and marries Ruth. Upon Brown's death, his will is read in which there is a provision making Ruth his beneficiary. May Ruth collect under the policy?

Answer No. A beneficiary can be changed only in the way prescribed by the policy. Even a clearly proved intention to make a change is not sufficient if the formal requirements are lacking.

Question Brown takes out a policy on his own life, payable to his brother, reserving to himself the power to change the beneficiary. After Brown's subsequent marriage, he writes to the company stating that he wishes to make his wife the beneficiary. A blank form is sent him for this purpose which he fills out and executes in the presence of a witness. However, Brown is suddenly taken ill and dies before the form with the policy is mailed to the company. Who is the beneficiary under his policy?

Answer The brother. At the time of his death, the company had not received the change of beneficiary; hence, Brown's brother would receive payment.

Question Jones takes out a life insurance policy, making his wife the beneficiary. The wife subsequently poisons Jones who dies. Who is entitled to payment on the policy?

Answer Jones' estate will get it all, the wife being excluded from taking any share.

Question May a life insurance policy be assigned for the benefit of creditors?

Answer Yes. Usually, this does not require the consent of the company.

Question An insurance company wrongfully cancels Brown's life insurance policy. What can Brown do?

Answer He can, through his lawyer, maintain an immediate action for damages. Most courts will allow him to recover all premiums paid, with interest from date of each payment; or, where Brown's health is such at the time of the breach that this measure of damages fails to compensate him for his loss, he may be given such sum as will enable him to procure a like policy in another company. Instead of bringing the action for damages, Brown may, through his counsel, bring an action to have the policy restored or put in effect. Finally, he can tender the premiums and await the maturity of the policy before action is begun

Advisory 6

CRIMINAL LAW

Crimes are divided into felonies and misdemeanors, the former being the most serious offenses against the State. In turn, felonies and misdemeanors are usually divided into crimes against the person, such as murder, rape and assault; and those against property, such as burglary, robbery and fraud. Measured in terms of offenders, crimes against property far exceed crimes against the person, in the ratio, probably, of ten to one. Altogether, more than three hundred and fifty thousand men, women and children are confined to penal and correctional institutions each year. But even this figure does not accurately reflect the appalling amount of crime we really have. Many criminals are never caught; many of those who are caught are never convicted; and of those convicted many are released on probation or given a suspended sentence. Criminologists believe that only ten percent of those committing major offenses are ever apprehended. Assuming that the same rate applies to petty crimes, this nation maintains an army of at least three million five hundred thousand criminals annually. Small wonder that our estimated yearly crime bill totals $13,000,000,000!

Without the restraining influence of a penal code, these figures would be even more shocking. Imagine what would happen if, overnight, the criminal law were abolished and men could commit crime without fear of punishment!

The maintenance of law and order, then, is of more than academic interest. Indeed, the very safety of our lives and the preservation of our property may depend, in the last analysis, upon the efficient enforcement of the penal code.

So grave is the stigma attached to anyone charged with crime that society has placed a number of safeguards around the accused. One of the most important is the legal presumption that every man is innocent until he is proved guilty.

This means that the burden of establishing guilt is on the prosecuting attorney. To further protect the defendant, the State, in whose name the prosecution is carried on, must prove the guilt. of the accused beyond a reasonable doubt. Where the evidence is conflicting and there is a reasonable doubt in the mind of the judge or jury, the defendant must be acquitted.

Question What is a crime?

Answer A crime is any act, or failure to act, punishable by law, either 1n the form of a fine and or imprisonment.

Question What is the chief difference between a criminal action and a civil one?

Answer A criminal proceeding is always prosecuted by the State and tried in the Criminal Court. A crime, therefore, is a wrong against the community or State, and is punishable as such. The form of the action is State of (blank) vs. John Doe. Upon conviction, the accused is given a fine and or imprisonment. A person who has been robbed, for example, causes the arrest of the accused and becomes the prosecuting witness for the State against the accused or defendant. He, the prosecuting witness, requires no lawyer, for the State undertakes, on his behalf, to prosecute the criminal, acting through its prosecuting attorney. A civil action, on the other hand, does not affect the community or State. It is an action of one individual against another. The usual form is John Doe, plaintiff, vs. John Smith, defendant. It is a proceeding brought to redress an unlimited variety of wrongs committed by one person against another. It may be a damage suit to secure money for injuries resulting from an accident, or damages for a breach of contract. On the other hand, it may be suit in "replevin," to recover a specific thing wrongfully in the possession of another—as, for example, furniture, after failure to pay the money due on it. It may be a suit in ejectment where the plaintiff does not seek damages but merely seeks to oust a tenant who has failed to pay his rent.

In all such cases, both the plaintiff and the defendant appear in court. Both parties require a lawyer to represent them, and it is usually good wisdom for the party having a legal paper served upon him to immediately consult his attorney so that he may be properly advised as to his rights and obligations. If, as a result of the proceedings, the plaintiff wins, he will usually obtain the particular end for which suit was brought. Should the defendant win, the case is dismissed unless, of course, the plaintiff takes an appeal.

Question   John walks on Jim's land wrongfully, but does not disturb the peace in doing so. Is this a crime or a civil injury?

Answer   A civil injury, since it does not affect the other members of the community as to require the State to punish John. John is merely liable in an action for damages.

Question   While strolling through the country, you spy a sign marked: "Stop. No Trespassing Under Penalty of the Law." Instead of stopping, you walk on the land. Have you committed a crime?

Answer   No, but you may be sued for damages.

Question   John, a grocer, cheats Mrs. Smith by giving a false weight to the sugar she buys. Is this a crime?

Answer   Yes. Here, the wrong affects the whole community to such an extent that the public welfare requires John be punished.

Question   What is treason?

Answer   Treason is the act of waging war against the United States, or giving its enemies aid or comfort. It is an offense committed usually during war and by a citizen of the country

Question   What is a felony?

Answer   It is a serious crime such as murder, manslaughter, rape, sodomy, robbery, larceny, arson, burglary and such other crimes as are made felonies expressly by law.

Question   What is a misdemeanor?

Answer   A misdemeanor is a crime that is neither treason nor a felony. It is generally a less serious offense, such as disturbing the peace, drunkenness, disorderly conduct, conducting a house of ill fame, assault and battery, etc. The punishment is usually, but not always, less severe than in felonies

Question   Why is it important to know the difference between a felony and a misdemeanor?

Answer   In felonies, there may be principals and accessories. In misdemeanors, all are principals and can be punished as such. Again, unintentionally causing death in committing some felony robbery, for example is murder, while to unintentionally cause death in committing a misdemeanor assault and battery, for example is manslaughter, a less serious crime. A warrant is unnecessary in making an arrest for a felony. It is usually necessary to authorize arrest for a misdemeanor. Moreover, in making an arrest for a felony, the accused may be killed if he cannot otherwise be taken. This is not true in the case of a misdemeanor.

Question   A publisher prints and circulates an obscene book, for which he is arrested by the postal authorities. In his defense, he pleads that his motives in publishing the book were good in that he desired to correct abuses in intercourse between the sexes. May he still be convicted of sending obscene matter through the mail, a Federal offense?

Answer   Yes. The law is unconcerned with motives in the commission of crimes, be they good or bad. The reason for. this is simple: if a good motive or reason served as a defense, all a murderer would have to show to gain an acquittal would be that the victim was a bad character and that the world was better off for being rid of him. The law does not tolerate such a point of view.

Question   Andrew parks his car within fifteen feet of a fireplug, not knowing that parking within twenty feet is forbidden. At the traffic court hearing, he pleads ignorance of the law. Is this a defense?

Answer   No. Ignorance of the law excuses no one. Legally, each person is presumed to know the law. Otherwise, persons could escape the consequence of their acts by pleading or pretending such ignorance.

Question   A blind man sells obscene literature. In his defense he pleads that he did not know that the magazine he is selling is obscene. Is that a good defense?

Answer   Yes. Here, the point is that the blind man might not actually know the magazine is obscene. Of course, if it could be shown by other testimony that he did know, then he would be found guilty. Ignorance of the law is not here involved; only ignorance of fact—in this case that the blind man did not and could not know what he was selling.

Question   John takes Henry's watch in the belief that it belongs to him. May John be found guilty of larceny?

Answer   No. A reasonable and honest mistake of fact will excuse the defendant.

Question   Is a married woman responsible for the crimes she commits?

Answer Yes. She is criminally responsible for any offense committed of her own free will. She is not responsible, however, for crimes, other than treason or murder, committed under pressure of her husband.

Question To what extent is a child responsible for his crimes?

Answer Under the age of seven a child cannot be convicted of any crime. Between the ages of seven and fourteen it is legally presumed that the child is incapable of committing a crime, but this presumption may be rebutted by the prosecuting attorney by showing that the child had sufficient intelligence and understanding to comprehend the nature of the crime. Children over fourteen are as much responsible for their criminal acts as adults. To escape responsibility, the child has the burden of satisfying the jury that he did not have sufficient client intelligence to understand the nature and consequence of his act.

Question To what extent are insane persons relieved of responsibility for their criminal acts?

Answer A man is not criminally responsible for an act if, by reason of mental infirmity, he is incapable of distinguishing between right and wrong with respect to the particular act. Some courts hold, moreover, that a man is not criminally responsible if he is driven to the act by an irresistible impulse, even though he knows such act to be wrong.

Question A father believes that God has appeared before him, commanding him to kill his child as a sacrifice, which he does. Is the father guilty of murder?

Answer No. Here, he is acting under an insane delusion and would not be held responsible for the killing.

Question To what extent is drunkenness an excuse for crime?

Answer Generally, it is no excuse.

Question Herman plans to commit robbery and tells Joe about it. Joe informs the police who come to arrest Herman. Is such an arrest lawful?

Answer No; The mere intent to commit a crime, unaccompanied by the crime itself, is not punishable.

Question John urges you to commit a crime, which you refuse to do. May John be punished criminally?

Answer Yes. Soliciting a person to commit a crime, even though the crime is not carried out, is punishable by law, on grounds of public policy. This is done to discourage the commission of crimes.

Question   A man seizes a woman with intent to rape, but voluntarily changes his mind and refrains from doing so. Of what crime, if any, is he guilty?

Answer   Attempt to rape, a less serious offense than rape itself, though often punishable almost as severely. This problem is to be distinguished from the problem in Question 19 in that here the attempt has already been made and assault committed.

Question   Three men agree to commit a crime. Later, two of the men abandon the scheme, but the third commits the crime formerly agreed upon by all three. When the latter is arrested, he reveals the identities of the other two men. They, in turn, plead that they had given up any idea of committing the crime and had not taken part. Can the two men be prosecuted?

Answer   Yes, for conspiracy. In a conspiracy it does not matter at all whether the act agreed upon is carried out or not. The crime is committed when two or more people conspire to commit an unlawful act. Of course, while technically they would be convicted of conspiracy, their punishment. would be less severe than that of the criminal who actually commits the crime.

Question   While in a department store, Mrs. Smith is stopped by a store detective who accuses her of stealing a pair of hose. Despite her denials, and over her protests, he insists on taking her to his office in the store where he causes her to be searched. No stockings are found upon her person. In all, Mrs. Smith has been detained about ten minutes against her will, and is finally released with the apologies of the store detective. What can she do about this?

Answer   She may cause the arrest of the detective for false imprisonment and sue the department store for damages for causing the false imprisonment. The detective is the agent for the store; his unlawful acts, when performed within the scope of his authority, will bind his principal, the owner of the store. The crime consists in depriving a person of his freedom of movement, without legal authority and against his will. The place of imprisonment is unimportant. Arresting the wrong person under a warrant is also false imprisonment, as is an arrest by an officer without a warrant when a warrant is necessary. An arrest by an officer, where the officer has no authority, also constitutes the crime. When a person is falsely imprisoned, he may not only cause the arrest of the officer, but may also sue him for damages.

Question What is homicide?

Answer It is the killing of one human being by another. It includes murder and manslaughter.

Question What is murder?

Answer Murder is the unlawful killing of a human being with malice aforethought, either express or implied.

Question Upon the prolonged disappearance of John's wife, John is arrested for her murder. The body is never found or accounted for. May John be convicted?

Answer No. It is not enough to show merely that the body is missing; there must be direct proof of death.

Question What is the difference between murder in the first degree and murder in the second degree?

Answer In most states, murder in the first degree is established upon proof that there is an actual intent to kill, with premeditation; or where the slaying is committed, though unintentionally, in the performance of such crimes as arson, rape, robbery or burglary. Thus, a burglar, surprised in the act of robbery, who shoots and kills, is guilty of murder in the first degree, even though the killing was done without premeditation. Murder in the first degree is generally punishable by death or life imprisonment. Murder in the second degree is usually the unlawful killing of a human being without premeditation, and is less serious than murder in the first degree.

Question Mr. Brown kills his wife, having plotted to do so in order to collect on her insurance. Of what crime is he guilty?

Answer Murder in the first degree, since the killing is premeditated.

Question Coming home unexpectedly, a husband finds his wife in the arms of another man. He shoots the stranger. Of what crime is he guilty?

Answer Probably second degree murder, for the slaying was committed in the heat of passion but without premeditation.

Question John and his sweetheart agree to commit suicide. John kills his sweetheart but, losing his nerve, doesn't kill himself. What crime has John committed?

Answer Murder, probably in the first degree, since there is a legal presumption against suicide; in the absence of proof of such a fact, the law would presume both malice and premeditation. If a suicide note were produced, it probably would reduce the crime to murder in the second degree.

Question What is the difference between murder and manslaughter?

Answer The chief distinction is that in murder the killing is committed with premeditated malice, while in manslaughter the killing is without malice or premeditation. Manslaughter is a less serious crime than either first or second degree murder.

Question What is voluntary manslaughter?

Answer This is an intentional killing, in sudden passion or heat of, blood caused by a reasonable provocation, and without malice aforethought. To reduce a crime from murder to man slaughter, the killing must be without malice, even though intentional. The provocation must be so great as to reasonably excite passion in an ordinary man, causing him to act rashly and without reflection. There is sufficient provocation to reduce a crime to manslaughter when one kills after being assaulted violently or with great rudeness; when an unlawful attempt is made to arrest one; when the killing is in mutual combat, provided no unfair advantage is taken by the slayer, and the occasion was not sought for the purpose of killing; where a husband catches his wife in adultery and kills her or her lover. Of course, the same applies in the case of a wife who kills her husband or his mistress. But provocation does not reduce murder to manslaughter? the passion has actually cooled by the time the blow is struck or if there has been a reasonable time for cooling. Both these questions are facts to be weighed by the jury.

Question What is criminal negligence?

Answer It is acting in such a reckless and dangerous manner as to constitute an utter disregard for human life. A railroad engineer who operates and wrecks his train while drunk is guilty of such negligence.

Question Jim, who is drunk, drives his car so recklessly that he runs it on the sidewalk, striking a pedestrian who shortly afterwards dies from his injuries. Of what crime is Jim guilty?

Answer Manslaughter. Jim has acted so recklessly and with such willful disregard for human life as to convict him of this crime. Since there was no premeditation or malice, the crime would not be murder. Ordinarily, the killing of a pedestrian by an automobilist is not even manslaughter—unless the State can prove that the driver was negligent.

Question   Jim, a farmer, carelessly permits his bull to roam loose, the animal attacking a stranger and killing him. Of what crime is Jim guilty?

Answer   Manslaughter—since Jim's conduct in allowing a dangerous animal to be at large indicates a disregard for human life.

Question   As a lark, John calls out "Fire" in a crowded theater. Two people are killed and several injured because of the resulting panic. Will John be convicted of any crime?

Answer   Yes, manslaughter, at the very least. There is a possibility that he might be convicted of murder in the second degree, since John displayed a reckless disregard for human life, the law assuming malice on his part.

Question   A woman goes to a drugstore, purchasing a drug with which to commit an abortion on herself. She dies as a result of the drug and the medicine is traced back to the druggist. What crime has he committed?

Answer   Probably manslaughter, since he aided, though unwittingly, in bringing about her death. His crime would not b murder because of the absence of premeditation or malice.

Question   A midwife performs an abortion on Jane, resulting in Jane's death. With what crime can the midwife be charged?

Answer   Manslaughter—for the same reason as above.

Question   John engages in a fist fight with Harry in which Harry is knocked to the ground, his head striking the pavement, Harry suffers a severe head injury and dies thirteen months later from the effects thereof. John is tried for manslaughter. Can he be convicted?

Answer   No. To obtain a conviction, death must come within year and a day after the blow is struck or other act done; otherwise, the law conclusively presumes that death resulted from some other cause.

Question   A son learns that his mother is living in adultery with another man. In a fit of passion he seeks out and kills him. Has he committed a crime?

Answer   Yes, probably manslaughter.

Question   A burglar attempts to break into your house for the purpose of theft. May you kill him to prevent his entry?

Answer   Yes, such killing is justified to prevent the commission of a serious crime—in this case, burglary.

Question Under what circumstances is a person justified in killing another in "self-defense?"

Answer To make a killing justifiable or excusable on the ground of self-defense, it must reasonably appear that there is immediate danger of death or of great bodily harm. The danger, however, need not necessarily be real but must be believed, on reasonable grounds, to be real. In a sudden assault or fight, for example, the party threatened must retreat as far as he can with safety before taking his opponent's life. Finally, the slayer, in order to be excused on the ground of self-defense, must not have provoked the difficulty nor have been the aggressor.

Question While having a drink in a tavern, you are attacked by a drunk who, without provocation, slashes at you with a knife. You pick up a beer bottle and strike him over the head with it. The drunk falls to the ground, strikes his head against the bar rail, and dies. Can you be convicted of any crime?

Answer No. One attacked by a deadly weapon may assume that the intention is to kill and may kill in order to protect his own life.

Question In the above example, suppose that the drunk merely strikes you in the face. Are you justified in killing him?

Answer No, but you may return blow for blow.

Question While using an ax to chop wood, the head of the ax flies off, striking and killing a bystander. What crime has been committed?

Answer None. This is a case of "excusable" homicide, i.e., it involves the killing of another in the doing of a lawful act, without any intent to hurt and without criminal negligence. If, however, the owner knows that the head is loose and that it is likely to come off, he might be convicted of manslaughter, for he will then have revealed a reckless and criminal disregard for human life.

Question Under what circumstances is one justified in taking another's life?

Answer 1. In the performance of a public duty; as, for example, a hangman executing a criminal in accordance with law.
2. When a peace officer or private person kills another to prevent commission of a serious crime.
3. When a police officer attempts to arrest a criminal for a serious crime and the criminal tries to escape; or when the

criminal attempts to escape after his arrest but while in custody.

4. When a person who, without fault, kills his attacker to save himself from death or great bodily harm.

Question   John is arrested for robbery and, eluding the policeman, makes an escape. The policeman draws his gun, killing John. Is the policeman guilty of any crime?

Answer   No. An officer may kill to prevent an escape, if such extreme measures are necessary.

Question   Suppose John is arrested for fighting and attempts to escape. May the policeman kill to prevent the escape?

Answer   No. Where one is arrested for a minor crime and does not assault the officer, the policeman may not kill but must let him escape.

Question   John comes home one evening to find his wife being raped. May he legally kill the ravisher?

Answer   Yes. One is justified in killing to prevent the commission of a serious crime, in this case, rape.

Question   John comes home one afternoon to find his wife in bed with a stranger. The intercourse is voluntary. May John kill the stranger?

Answer   No. Killing is not justified where the sexual act is free and voluntary. John would probably be convicted of manslaughter, not murder, since there is an absence of premeditation and malice, the crime being committed in a sudden heat of passion caused by understandable provocation.

Question   What is larceny?

Answer   This is taking and carrying away of the personal goods of another of any value from any place with the criminal or fraudulent intent to steal the same.

Question   What is the difference between grand and petty larceny?

Answer   The difference is chiefly in the value of the article stolen. Many statutes provide that stolen articles under the value of $10 to $25 are to be considered petty larcenies and punished as misdemeanors. Articles above a stated value are considered more serious and are termed grand larcenies, punishable as felonies.

Question   A maid takes a pair of stockings from her employer without the latter's knowledge. What crime has she committed?

Answer   Larceny, since she unlawfully took goods belonging to another person.

Question Tom drops a false coin into a vending machine and receives a package of cigarettes. What crime has he committed?

Answer Larceny, since he unlawfully took goods belonging to another person.

Question What is embezzlement?

Answer This is the misappropriation of funds or goods that come into a person's hands lawfully. For example, Jim, a collector for an insurance company, collects money due the company; but, instead of turning it over to the company, he pockets it himself. Since the money came legally into Jim's hands, it is not larceny. When Jim failed to turn over the money to the company, he misappropriated it and hence committed the crime of embezzlement.

Question How does embezzlement differ from larceny?

Answer In embezzlement, the original taking is lawful. In larceny, it is not.

Question What is the crime of obtaining money or property under false pretenses?

Answer It is such a fraudulent representation of fact, by one knowing it to be false, as to induce a person to whom it is made to part with something of value. For example, Mrs. Jones goes to a department store to buy a fur coat. She tells the salesperson to charge it to Mrs. Smith, saying that she is Mrs. Smith and signing the charge slip in that name. Mrs. Jones can be prosecuted for obtaining goods by false pretenses.

Question A man obtains board and lodging at a hotel by falsely telling the proprietor that he expects a check at a certain time. Is he guilty of the crime of false pretenses?

Answer No. A statement as to future events, or a statement of intention or expectation, is not a false pretense. A mere promise. a mere expression of opinion or belief, or mere dealer's talk are other acts not considered false pretenses.

Question On the strength of his promise to marry her, Mr. Jones gives Tom $1,000. Tom refuses to go through with his bargain and Mrs. Jones causes his arrest. Can he be convicted of obtaining money under false pretenses?

Answer No. Statements or promises as to future events are not sufficient to sustain a conviction. The false pretense must relate to an existing fact. Mrs. Jones can probably recover the money, however, in a civil suit.

Question A customer asks a grocer for a pound of sugar. After receiving the bag, the customer protests that it seems to weigh less than a pound. The grocer insists that it is the full measure. When he arrives home, the customer weighs the sugar and discovers that it weighs less than a pound. Is the grocer guilty of any crime?

Answer   No, not unless the bag was actually weighed out to the customer. If, however, by using a false weight, the grocer gives the customer less than the full measure, the grocer may be convicted of cheating. This is also true where the grocer places his hand on the scale to give false weight.

Question   John gives Bill a check for $50. When Bill presents the check to the bank it is returned marked "insufficient funds." Has John committed a crime?

Answer   No, not if John had any funds at all on deposit. Even if they were insufficient to cover the check, he could only be sued civilly, not criminally.

Question   Harry gives Bill a check for merchandise in the sum of $50. The check is returned by the bank marked "no such so count." Of what crime can Harry be convicted?

Answer   Obtaining goods under false pretenses.

Question   Entering a restaurant, a man orders and eats a meal. At the time, he has no money to pay for it. Has he committed a crime?

Answer   No. A person is not guilty of the crime of obtaining goods under false pretenses when there is only a failure to disclose facts-in this case, the lack of money. He can only be sued for the amount of the meal.

Question   What is robbery?

Answer   Robbery is the taking and carrying away of the personal property of another, from his person or in his presence, by fear or violence. It is larceny plus force. When one man picks another's pocket, the crime is larceny. When he does so at the point of a gun, why a threat to kill or otherwise perform serious bodily harm, the offense is robbery. Robbery is usually punished more severely than larceny.

Question   John robs a filling station of $150. That same night, feeling repentant, he returns the money to the owner. Can he be convicted of robbery?

Answer   Yes. A person committing a robbery cannot escape responsibility by repenting and abandoning or returning the property.

Question   A man knocks a purse out of a woman's hand, picks it up from the ground and runs off with it. Has he committed larceny or robbery?

Answer   Larceny. To commit robbery, sufficient force must be used to overcome resistance. If there is any injury to the owner, or if she resists the attempt to rob her and her resistance is overcome, there is sufficient violence to make the taking robbery.

Question   What is the crime of receiving stolen property?

Answer   This is the receiving of goods when knowing or believing them to be stolen.

Question   A pawnbroker is offered a quantity of jewelry by a shabbily dressed stranger for a ridiculously low price. The pawnbroker buys the jewels. Later, they turn out to have been stolen. May the pawnbroker be prosecuted for receiving stolen goods?

Answer   Yes. The law assumes that, at the time the jewels were bought, the pawnbroker should have known they were stolen. This is so because of the great difference between the value of the articles and the price paid for them, also, the unlikelihood of the person selling them being the lawful owner.

Question   What is forgery?

Answer   Forgery is the false writing, or alteration of writing, with the intent to defraud. Paintings, documents, checks, etc., may be the subject matter of this crime.

Question   John raises the amount of a check from $5 to $500 by altering the figures on the check. What is the crime?

Answer   Forgery.

Question   What is burglary?

Answer   Burglary is the breaking and entering of the dwelling house of another, at night, with intent to commit a serious crime. However, many states, by special law, have broadened burglary to include shops, stores, warehouses, etc., and have included burglary as being the breaking and entering in the daytime as well as the night.

Question   Bill forces open a locked window of a house at night. He enters and takes away with him a quantity of money. Of what crime is he guilty?

Answer   Burglary.

Question   John, the owner of a house, locks it up and leaves it, without intending to return. In his absence, the house is broken into and a quantity of goods are wrongfully removed.

Has burglary been committed?

Answer   No. When John left the house without intending to return, the house lost its character as a dwelling house. If he had only left temporarily, with the intention of returning, even though he remained away for some time, the house was a dwelling and a breaking and entry would be burglary. In this example, the crime committed was larceny, a less serious crime than burglary.

Question   A man sees the door of a house open, walks in and steals a quantity of goods. Has a burglary been committed?

Answer   No. In going through the open door no legal "breaking" has taken place. The crime committed is larceny. However. there need not be an actual breaking to constitute burglary. If a person gets into a house by some trick or fraud, with intent to commit a crime, there is a legal breaking and he is guilty of burglary.

Question   Suppose a window, being partly open, is pushed further open in order to make an entry. Is this burglary?

Answer   No, it is larceny. No "breaking" has taken place.

Question   What is arson?

Answer   Arson is the willful and malicious burning of the dwelling house of another. By state law, the offense has been broadened to include the burning of other buildings such as shops, warehouses, unoccupied houses, etc., and sometimes the burning of one's own house.

Question   In a political campaign, one of the candidates writes and circulates a pamphlet attacking his opponent as being "nothing but a cheap crook" who should be in jail rather than running for office. As a matter of fact, there is no truth to the charge. Is the writer guilty of any crime?

Answer   Yes, criminal libel, which is any published writing exposing a person to ridicule, hatred or contempt.

Question   Suppose, in the above example, the charges were two. would he still be guilty of criminal libel?

Answer   No, not if it appeared that the written attack was made in the public interest and for the public good.

Question   While on the witness stand and under oath, John testifies that he saw a certain automobile accident. Later, it is brought out by clear and convincing evidence that John was far from the scene at the time. Is John guilty of any crime?

Answer   Yes. Perjury. To be convicted of this crime, the perjurer mast testify, tinder oath, to a fact which he knows or believes to be false. The false testimony, moreover, must be important to the issue or dispute.

Question   Is perjury committed only in court?

Answer   No. Perjury may be committed in making a false oath in procuring a marriage license; in naturalization proceedings, in an event where one is required, etc.

Question   A lawyer instructs his client to take the witness stand and swear falsely to some important fact. What crimes have been committed?

Answer   The client is guilty of perjury and the attorney of "subornation of perjury"—which is persuading another to testify falsely under oath.

Question   Bill, a bank teller, embezzles $5,000 from the bank where he is employed. The president of the bank informs Bill that if he returns the bulk of the money stolen, he will see that Bill is not prosecuted. Is such an agreement legal?

Answer   No. The president of the bank may be found guilty of "compounding" a crime; he may be sentenced to prison, since it is unlawful for one person, for any valuable consideration, to enter into an agreement not to prosecute another for a crime.

Question   What is bigamy?

Answer   This crime is committed when a person, already legally married, marries another person during the life of his or her wife or husband. Many states, by law, allow remarriages where the husband or wife has been continually absent for a specified period, usually seven years.

Question   May a man be found guilty of raping a prostitute?

Answer   Yes. The fact, however, that a woman is a prostitute, or is even promiscuous, is always considered by the court in determining the question of consent, the court taking the view, usually, that such a woman is more likely to consent than either a virgin or anyone previously enjoying a good reputation.

Question   James takes Alice out for an automobile ride. He gets her intoxicated. While she is in that condition, he has sexual intercourse with her. Is he guilty of any crime?

Answer   Yes, rape. A really drunken woman cannot consent to intercourse. Upon recovering her senses, she may have the man charged with the crime.

Question   Charles persuades Janet, a virgin, to have sexual intercourse with him, promising to marry her if she does. Relying on this promise, Janet agrees. Charles later changes his mind and refuses to go through with the marriage ceremony. What may Janet do about it?

Answer   She may have Charles prosecuted for the crime of seduction. If, however, at any time before the trial Charles agrees to marry her, there can be no prosecution and the case will be dropped. It is not one of the more serious offenses.

Question   What is habeas corpus?

Answer   This is a writ issued by a court to determine whether a person detained in custody is being held legally. It is frequently used to secure a hearing where one is detained or incarcerated as a lunatic, criminal or juvenile delinquent. The function of the writ is to inquire whether the detention itself. is legal. If the imprisonment is illegal, the court will discharge the prisoner. The application for the writ of habeas corpus is usually made by the prisoner's lawyer.

Question   A husband has his wife committed to an insane asylum when, in fact, she is quite rational, hoping thereby to obtain control of her property. How may her release be secured?

Answer   By applying for a writ of habeas corpus. At the hearing, the court will determine whether or not she is actually insane.

Question   Without having been served with a warrant, John is arrested and convicted of a crime. It turns out later that John's arrest was unlawful in that a warrant was necessary for his arrest. How may this point be brought up, after John's conviction and imprisonment?

Answer   By a writ of habeas corpus.

Question   John, a married man, is inducted into the army service of the United States. While in the army, John accuses the Selective Service Board of having drafted him before it had exhausted the supply of single men. How may he test the validity of his induction?

Answer   By having his lawyer apply for a writ of habeas corpus.

Question   Mrs. Brown's servant, Alice, lets her boyfriend into her employer's home for the purpose of robbing it. Alice is away while the house is being robbed. Is she guilty of any crime?

Answer   Yes. She is guilty of being an accessory before the fact, this being one who aids or brings about the commission of a. serious crime, although absent when the crime is actually committed. Had Alice been present, she too would have been guilty of robbery.

Question John urges George to kill Bill by shooting him. Instead, George kills Bill by stabbing him. Of what crime, if any, is John guilty?

Answer John is guilty of being an accessory before the fact to murder, just as he would have been if George had followed John's instruction to shoot Bill.

Question Is an accessory before the fact punished as severely as the actual criminal?

Answer Yes, usually.

Question Tom, having committed a burglary, is sought by the police. He seeks refuge with Harry who, after hearing about the crime, gives Tom food and shelter for the night. The next morning, the police break in and arrest both Tom and Harry. Of what crime is Harry guilty?

Answer Harry is guilty of being an accessory after the fact, this being one who, knowing a serious crime to have been committed by another, receives or otherwise aids him in order to help him escape punishment.

Question In the above question, assume that Harry did not know Tom had committed a serious crime. Would he still be guilty of being an accessory after the fact?

Answer No. The person giving aid must know that a serious crime has been perpetrated.

Question Jack rushes into Mabel's apartment, confessing that the police are after him for robbery. He tells her he needs money with which to make a getaway. Mabel gives him $50. Jack leaves. Shortly afterwards, the police arrive and, after questioning, Mabel admits that she gave Jack some money to get rid of him. Technically, what crime has Mabel committed?

Answer Unless she insists that she did not know Jack had committed robbery, Mabel would be found guilty of being an accessory after the fact.

Question Is an accessory after the fact punished as severely as the actual criminal?

Answer The punishment is less severe, usually.

Question May only police officers make arrests?

Answer No. Any person may arrest another, without a warrant, when he sees a serious crime committed or where a dangerous wound is incited in his presence. Anyone may arrest and restrain those involved in fights or brawls; Anyone may arrest another whom be reasonably suspects to have committed a serious crime, actually committed.

Question A riot takes place in a defense plant. Is John, a mere spectator, under any obligation to help suppress it?

Answer Yes. When requested he must aid police officers to suppress the riot. This applies even to fights between two or more persons.

Question Under what circumstances may policemen make an arrest without a warrant?

Answer Without a warrant, they may arrest persons committing any crime in their presence, as well as those whom they reasonably suspect to have committed a serious crime. In brawls, officers may not only arrest and bring the offenders before a magistrate, but may, upon their own authority; imprison them for a reasonable time.

Question You are arrested for having stolen an automobile and are placed in jail pending your trial. How may you secure your release before trial?

Answer By getting someone to go your bails—meaning that a responsible person, or a professional bondsman, puts up property before the court or magistrate as a guaranty that you will appear at the place of trial to answer the charge against you.

Question May bail be offered in all cases?

Answer Yes, except in cases where the penalty may be death; as for example, murder, rape, treason and, in some states, arson.

Question What happens if the accused, released temporarily on bail, fails to show up for the trial?

Answer The bondsman loses his money. Moreover, the accused may be rearrested with the likelihood that, upon conviction, his punishment will be much more severe.

Question May a witness to a crime be jailed pending trial of the accused?

Answer Yes. State witnesses may be required to furnish bond for their appearance and, if they cannot do so, may be committed to jail until the actual trial is held.

Question John is in jail, charged with the commission of a serious crime. While asleep, he utters words confessing his guilt; the words are taken down by the jailer. May this "confession" be introduced at the trial?

Answer No. Words spoken in sleep or during the delirium of illness are not admissible.

Question Henry threatens to "knock Jack's block off," but actually does nothing. Is Henry guilty of any crime?

Answer No, not unless the threat carries with it a reasonable fear that it will be executed. If Jack is under such fear, Henry may be arrested for assault.

Question Suppose Henry actually does strike Jack. What crime has he then committed?

Answer Assault and battery.

Question Tom angrily spits at Bill. May Tom be arrested?

Answer Yes, for the crime of assault and battery. It is also a crime to push another angrily out of the way.

Question A younger person tells an older man that "if you were not an old man I would knock you down." Has the younger man committed a crime?

Answer No, since the words indicate that no injury will be indicted.

Question A school teacher slaps an unruly child. Is the teacher guilty of any offense?

Answer No not if the punishment is moderate.

Question Joan is placed by the court in the custody of her mother. The father, without the mother's consent or permission, takes Joan on a trip. Is the father guilty of any crime?

Answer Yes, kidnapping.

Question Susan runs away from her father's home, seeking refuge in the home of a friend in another city. Is the friend guilty of any crime for harboring her?

Answer No.

Question Alice's boyfriend persuades her to leave home without the consent of her parents and to run away with him. Alice is underage. Is her boyfriend guilty of any offense?

Answer Yes, the crime of abduction, a less serious crime than kidnapping.

Advisory 7

LANDLORD AND TENANT

The law of landlord and tenant is another extension of the principles of contract and is governed, more or less, by the same rules. Just as an employment contract, for example, contains the terms agreed upon by the employer and employee, so the lease embodies the terms agreed to by the landlord and tenant, the breach of which may give rise to a suit for damages.

A contract, it will be recalled, must have a lawful consideration and a definite subject matter. In the landlord-tenant relationship, the consideration is the rent paid by one party to the other, the subject matter being the rented, or "demised," premises. A lease itself is the grant of a right to the exclusive possession of land for a definite term less than that which the grantor has in the land. An example of this is where one, owning a piece of property absolutely, or, as it is technically called, in "fee simple," leases it to another for a shorter term—for instance, ten years.

Question   Who are the parties to a lease?

Answer   The lessor and the lessee, the former being the one renting the premises, the latter the one to whom the premises are rented.

Question   In writing or drawing a lease, where a lawyer is not available, what points should be included?

Answer   A lease should contain the names and addresses of the parties; the consideration, price or rent of the premises to be leased, a description of the premises to be leased, with whatever exceptions and reservations agreed by the parties, the terms and period for which the property is to be leased, the purpose for which the property is to be leased and, lastly, a clause providing for the landlord's re-entry on non-payment of rent or other non-performance of covenants on the part of the tenant, and, of course, the signature of the parties to the lease.

Question Is a lease made on Sunday binding?

Answer No.

Question You give a deposit on an apartment or house and later change your mind about it, demanding the return of your deposit from the owner. Must he return it to you?

Answer No.

Question You sign a lease for one year for an apartment and, as evidence of your good faith, give a deposit. Under the terms of the lease, you are not to move in until three weeks after the signing thereof. A few days after the lease is signed, you ask the landlord to return your deposit because you have decided the apartment is not adequate for your needs. Is the landlord under obligation to return your deposit?

Answer No. The landlord not only need not return your deposit—he can also sue you for breach of contract of the entire lease, holding you liable for the year's rent.

Question When is rent due?

Answer Rent is usually due in advance.

Question If rent falls due on a Sunday, must it be paid that day?

Answer No. It may be paid the next business day. However, if it falls due on any other holiday it must be paid that day.

Question If a lease begins on the second day of January, rent commencing from that day, when is the next rent due, assuming it is payable monthly?

Answer February 1st.

Question Where a lease provides that rent is to be payable either quarterly or monthly who determines when it shall be paid?

Answer The landlord.

Question A tenant, by a written lease, agrees to pay $60 per month for the use of the rented premises. Later, he persuades the landlord to reduce the rent to $50 monthly. After taking the reduced rental for several months, the landlord changes his mind, and now tells the tenant that the rent is again $60 per month. May the tenant refuse to pay the original rent?

Answer No. There is no legal consideration for the reduced rental.

Question A tenant requests his landlord to reduce the rent because of the inconvenience and expense suffered by him during the making of repairs. The landlord agrees. Later, the landlord changes his mind. May the tenant continue to pay the reduced rent?

Answer   Yes. There is now a legal consideration for the reduction, binding on the landlord.

Question   Can a tenant refuse to pay rent where the plumbing and drainage are defective, although no provision in the lease is made therefor?

Answer   No. Nor may a tenant refuse to pay rent if the house is infected or unhealthful.

Question   Though the lease provides for it, the landlord consistently fails to supply adequate heat. Does this justify a refusal to pay rent?

Answer   Yes. The same applies to the landlord's failure to comply with his agreement to furnish water or light. The tenant may also sue for breach of contract. Of course, notice should be given the landlord in order to provide him an opportunity to make good the alleged defects.

Question   John's house, which he has rented from Bill, is temporarily made unsuitable for occupancy, due to the making of repairs by the landlord. May John refuse to pay rent until such time as the house is once again habitable?

Answer   No. If, however, the landlord fails to exercise diligence in carrying repairs through to completion, thus depriving the tenant of the use of the premises, he may be entitled to suspend payment of rent.

Question   Not long after you rent a house, a bowling alley is erected adjacent to it. The noise from the bowling alley prevents you from sleeping at night. May you break your lease and avoid payment of rent due under it?

Answer   Yes. With the rental of premises there is an implied covenant that the tenant will have "the quiet enjoyment" of these premises, meaning simply that he will not be disturbed in his use of the property. When, as in the above case, something occurs which disturbs the tenant's "quiet enjoyment," he may vacate the premises and file suit for breach of his lease.

Question   You rent a store, signing a lease for a year, with an option to renew. At the end of six months, prior to the expiration of the lease, you find that the business you do does not warrant your staying and you move from the store. What rent will you be liable for?

Answer   You will be liable for the remaining six months on the lease.

If the owner succeeds in re-renting the store, your obligation will be reduced proportionately. If the lease you signed is for five years and you stay for only six months, you will be liable for four-and-a-half years' rent.

Question Bill leases a drugstore. It is provided that the landlord shall give his written consent when Bill applies for a liquor license. After Bill takes over the store, the landlord changes his mind and willfully refuses to give his consent. May Bill refuse to pay his rent?

Answer Yes, if he abandons the premises. Bill could then file suit against the landlord for breach of contract.

Question You rent a store for a period of one year, rent to be paid in twelve equal monthly installments. As required by your lease, you give the landlord written notice of your intention not to renew the lease. Instead of moving the day your lease expires, you continue to stay on for another week or so. What can the landlord do?

Answer He can continue to treat you as a tenant "holding over," compelling you to continue payment of rent for an additional year. Or he can sue you as a trespasser—that is, as one wrongfully in possession of his property.

Question A tenant in an apartment house is unable to pay his rent. May the landlord seize a piano in the tenant's apartment, sell it and, from the proceeds, take out the rent due?

Answer Yes. Many, if not all, states have laws which provide, in substance, that a landlord may take goods and chattels on the rented premises. Other laws provide, however, that certain articles shall be exempt from such "distress."

Question Suppose, in the above case; the piano was subject to a mortgage. Could the landlord still take it?

Answer Yes, providing the landlord satisfies the mortgage— that is, pays off the debt due on it.

Question A tenant, without the landlord's knowledge, uses the leased premises for an illegal purpose, such as gambling or as a house of prostitution. When the landlord discovers the illegal purpose, what can he do?

Answer A number of states, by law, provide that, in such cases, the lease shall be void and the landlord may recover possession, even where the tenant has paid the rent in advance. In the absence of a state law, however, the landlord has no right to terminate the lease. He may sue merely for its breach or obtain an injunction prohibiting such illegal use.

Question   A landlord leases a house to a tenant who, with the knowledge of the landlord, uses it as a house of prostitution. The tenant refuses to pay rent and the landlord files suit to recover rent for the premises. May he?

Answer   No. Where the lease is made with the intention that the premises shall be used for an illegal purpose, the landlord cannot recover rent.

Question   Does your landlord have a right to enter your apartment without your permission?

Answer   Yes. He may enter to demand payment of rent, where due, to prevent waste, to do anything to save himself from liability for negligence in connection. with the premises. For example, an owner may, without the consent of his tenant, tear down walls where the building has become unfit and unsafe by reason of fire or other defect.

Question   Suppose a landlord, without either authority or permission, forces himself into the tenant's premises. What can be done?

Answer   For an unauthorized entry, a landlord may be sued for damages. The unauthorized entry is called a trespass.

Question   How much heat is a landlord required to furnish in an apartment?

Answer   Generally, an amount which will make the temperature of the rooms reasonably comfortable for the average person during the time the premises are usually occupied.

Question   After being in your rented house for a few months, the heating system becomes defective and is unable to furnish 60° Fahrenheit. The lease provides that the landlord shall furnish the heat. You have sublet a few rooms in your house but, because of the defective heating system, your tenants move out. What damages may you recover?

Answer   You may recover the expenses to which you have been put as a result of having to leave the house, and also the loss of rental of rooms which you sublet.

Question   In his lease, a landlord agrees to provide the premises with sufficient heat. As a result of his negligent failure to do so, the tenant contracts tuberculosis. May he hold the landlord liable?

Answer   Yes, if it can be proved that such neglect is the proximate cause of the tuberculosis, or made an already existing tubercular condition worse.

Question	You rent a barber shop. After being in possession for a few months, the landlord fails to provide hot water for use in your business. What can you do?
Answer	You may cancel the lease and tile suit for damages. What you will get by way of damages will be the difference between the rent agreed on in the lease and the rent the barber shop would bring without hot water. The damages, of course, would include only the period for which you were deprived of hot water.
Question	In renting an apartment the landlord assures you that the rooms are "clean." A few days after you move in, you discover that the apartment is overridden with huge. You seek to cancel the lease. May you do so?
Answer	No. A statement that an apartment or house is "clean" means only that it has been swept and scoured after the last tenant moved out. It is not a guaranty that the place is free of bugs or mice.
Question	You rent a house and, shortly after moving in, you notice that it is infested with rats to such an extent as to make the house unlivable. Can you cancel the lease?
Answer	Yes, providing you have not created the condition and have made every effort to destroy the rats.
Question	You rent an apartment or house, the lease being silent on the question as to who is to make repairs. A few months after you have been living in the apartment or house, the plumbing goes out of control. You ask the landlord to make the necessary repairs. He refuses. Is he right in refusing?
Answer	Yes. In the absence of an express agreement, the landlord is not bound to make ordinary repairs—nor is he bound to pay for such repairs made by the tenant.
Question	Suppose, in the above example, there is no lease; the apartment or house is rented on a monthly basis. Would the same rule hold true as to the tenant's liability for repairs?
Answer	Yes.
Question	The sidewalk in front of your house is defective. Must you or the landlord make the repairs?
Answer	You, in the absence of an express agreement to the contract.
Question	You rent a five-room apartment from John and, in turn, you sublet one of your rooms to Jack. The window in Jack's room becomes broken. Who must replace the window?
Answer	Jack, since he is the subtenant and you the tenant—unless

an express agreement has been made by you to assume the obligation.

Question A lease provides that the landlord agrees to keep the house in good repair. The tenant, at his. own expense, hires a caretaker to keep the walks clean, rake, mow and seed the grounds. May he recover such expenses from the landlord?

Answer No. Such work does not constitute repairs.

Question In a lease, a tenant agrees to keep the plumbing and heating plant in good repair. A few weeks after he takes over the property, the tenant discovers that the heating plant was defective when he rented the property. May he compel the landlord to make the necessary repairs?

Answer No, unless the landlord practiced some fraud or deception on the tenant by concealing the defect.

Question A tenant leases a motion picture house, agreeing in the lease to keep the theater in good repair. The theater, through no fault of the tenant's, is totally destroyed by fire. Who must rebuild, the tenant or landlord?

Answer The tenant. Keeping premises in repair has often been held to mean restoring the property after a fire.

Question A tenant leases a retail clothing store, the lease providing that the landlord is to make all necessary repairs. Shortly afterward, the plate-glass front is broken by burglars. The landlord refuses to make repairs. What can the tenant do?

Answer He can replace the front at his own expense and sue the landlord for reimbursement.

Question A lease by which you have rented a building provides that the landlord is to make the repairs. After a severe rain, the basement of your building is flooded; you call in a crew to clean out the mud and water, paying them out of your own pocket. You later notify the landlord that you wish to be reimbursed for the money you paid out, advising him that, under the lease, he is required to make the repairs. Upon the landlord's refusal to return you the money, you file suit. Can you recover?

Answer No. In order to recover, you must first give the landlord notice of the deed and provide him with an opportunity to do the necessary repairs. Failure to give him such notice and opportunity relieves the landlord of liability, even when the lease provides that the landlord shall make the repairs.

Question Though the lease does not mention the party who is to make the repairs, the landlord agrees to repair the tenant's roof.

In doing the work, however, the tenant's property is damaged by rain falling through openings negligently left by the landlord while doing the work. Is the landlord liable?

Answer   Yes. Although a landlord is not under any obligation to make repairs, if he does undertake to make them, he is liable for any injuries which may result to the tenant from the negligent manner in which the work is done.

Question Suppose, in the above example, the landlord has employed a work man to do the work instead of doing it himself. Would the landlord still be liable?

Answer   Yes, on the theory that the landlord controls or directs the work. The landlord, in turn, may recover against the one doing the work.

Question An office building is heated by the landlord's engines. As a result of the latter's negligence, the heating apparatus explodes, causing damage to your office. Is the landlord liable?

Answer   Yes. A landlord is liable for injuries to the tenant, as he is to any other person rightfully on the premises, caused by the farmer's neglect to remedy defects in, or by his improper management of appliances of which he retains control. Landlords have been held liable for injuries caused by leakage of water pipes or other plumbing attachments in their control, elevators carrying freight or passengers, dumb waiters and machinery transmitting power, etc.

Question A tenant who has leased a warehouse places therein a reasonable weight of goods, not suspecting that the floor structure cannot bear this weight. The floor gives way and the landlord seeks to hold the tenant liable. Can he?

Answer   No. The tenant would be liable for injuries caused by placing an unreasonable and extraordinary weight in the building. In this case, the weight was reasonably related to the structure of the floor; the tenant, therefore, would be absolved of responsibility.

Question A state law provides that a landlord shall maintain lights in the hallway of all apartment houses occupied by two or more families. As a result of the failure of the landlord to provide such lights, a tenant stumbles down the stairs and breaks a leg. Is the landlord liable for damages?

Answer   Yes. The tenant is under no obligation to install bulbs or lights in hallways. For any injuries sustained by him or his family, or persons coming upon the premises for business with or at the invitation of the tenant, the landlord would be held responsible.

Question   You rent an apartment, the lease being silent concerning who shall make repairs. Your mother-in-law, while visiting you for the first time, stumbles and falls as a result of a broken step. Can the landlord be held responsible?

Answer   No. A landlord who, without agreeing to repair, and without knowledge of hidden defects, is not liable for personal injuries sustained on the rented premises-unless the premises contained some defect known to the landlord at the time of the rental and not disclosed to or discovered by the tenant.

Question   Suppose, in the above example, the landlord agrees to repair the defective step after it is called to his attention and that, as a result of his negligent failure to so repair, the mother-in-law stumbles and falls. Is the landlord then liable?

Answer   Yes.

Question   You are living in a rented house. A stranger, walking by, slips and falls on the ice you have neglected to remove. Who is liable, the owner of the property or you?

Answer   You, unless there is an express agreement to the contract.

Question   A landlord rents an apartment with knowledge that the timbers in a floor are defective. A few weeks later, a member of your family falls through the rotted floor, sustaining injuries. Is the landlord responsible?

Answer   Yes. The rule is that if there is some hidden defect which is known to the landlord at the time the lease is made, but which is not apparent to the prospective tenant, the landlord is bound to inform the tenant. Failing to do so, he is liable for injuries sustained by the tenant or his family.

Question   Thompson leases a floor of a building to Jones for warehouse purposes, knowing it to be too weak to be safely used for such purposes. The door collapses, causing personal injuries to the tenant below and damage to his goods. Is Thompson or Jones liable in damages to the tenant?

Answer   Thompson, the landlord. One renting premises to be used for a particular purpose, having reason to believe that this use of the premises is likely to injure a stranger, is liable to such person.

Question   A market company leases you a meat stall, reserving control over the passageway. A customer stumbles over a defective plank in the passageway, sustaining personal injuries. Who is liable in damages, the market company or you?

Answer   The market company, since it reserved control of the passageway.

Question   Your lease provides that, at its expiration, you are to return the apartment to the landlord in as good a condition as when you received it, natural wear and tear excepted. When you vacate the apartment, you remove some of the fixtures and leave some of the windows broken. What can the landlord do?

Answer   He can sue you for breach of the lease and collect damages.

Question   A lease provides that the tenant is to make all repairs. The store leased is destroyed by fire. To what extent is the tenant obligated?

Answer   He is usually bound to rebuild the store. He will also be bound to rebuild where the premises are destroyed by lightning, flood or tornado. As a precaution, the tenant should always insert in a lease a clause relieving him from liability in such cases.

Question   In the absence of a contract to that effect, is the tenant under any obligation to insure the buildings and other improvements on the premises for the benefit of the landlord?

Answer   No, but it is generally a good idea to do so, since, in case of destruction of the premises, the tenant would be held liable.

Question   A lease provides that the tenant shall insure the buildings for the landlord's benefit. He takes out one policy for a year, but does not renew. A fire occurs after the expiration of the policy. Is the tenant liable?

Answer   Yes. He must keep the premises insured for the entire tenancy.

Question   In his lease, a tenant agrees to insure the buildings on the premises and, in case of loss, to apply the proceeds of the insurance to the restoration of the buildings. After the fire, he assigns his lease to a third party. Must the third party apply the proceeds of the insurance to the restoration of the building?

Answer   Yes.

Question   You lease premises, known as the Jones Building, and now wish to change the name to the Smith Building. May you do so without the consent of the landlord where there is no provision in the lease?

Answer Yes.

Question In the absence of a provision in the lease to the contrary, may a tenant sublease the premises without the consent of the landlord?

Answer Yes. Most written leases, however, contain a clause prohibiting subletting, except by and with the consent of the owner.

Question After you lease a store, you desire to cover the outside walls with signs advertising your business. Your landlord objects. The lease itself is silent about such signs. May you use the outside walls?

Answer Yes. A tenant is entitled to use the outside walls, unless there is an express agreement to the contrary. Of course, he cannot use the walls so as to injure the property, or for purposes inconsistent with the reasonable enjoyment of the property.

Question In the absence of an express agreement, may a tenant alter the premises without obtaining the consent of the landlord?

Answer A tenant generally has no right to make material or permanent alterations in the rented premises. When, however, a tenant has a long lease, he usually has the right to make such changes as the business established requires, provided the value of the building is not impaired.

Question A tenant leases a house and land, planting a number of trees, bushes and shrubs. At the expiration of his tenancy, he seeks to remove that which he has himself planted. May he?

Answer Yes. If planted by the tenant he may remove them.

Question What are the obligations of a tenant who rents farming land?

Answer He must use the land as such, see that no waste is permitted, that the land is farmed in a husbandlike manner, that the soil is not unnecessarily exhausted by negligent or improper tillage and that repairs are made.

Question You rent a stock farm from Jones. Who is entitled to the natural increase of the stock?

Answer In the absence of an agreement to the contrary, the increase belongs to the tenant.

Question Who is entitled to the fruit of the trees on leased land?

Answer The tenant.

Question	As between the landlord and tenant, who is entitled to the annual crop on leased property?
Answer	The tenant, providing the crop has ripened or is severed from the soil during the terms of the tenant's lease.
Question	John rents a house and barn where he keeps a number of horses. He tells the landlord that he may have the manure to be made at the barn if he furnishes the straw there. This the landlord refuses to do. Later, the landlord claims the entire manure. Who is entitled to it?
Answer	The tenant. Manure made in livery stables, or in buildings unconnected with agricultural property, belongs to the tenant, unless, of course, there is a contract to the contrary.
Question	John leases a piece of farm land from Hill. John is unable to pay his rent and Hill re-enters, taking possession of the premises. Who is entitled to the growing crop planted by the tenant?
Answer	Hill. John's rights are lost by non-payment of rent.
Question	At the expiration of his lease, a tenant farmer seeks to remove manure made during his tenancy and from his own crops. May he do so?
Answer	No. This is done as a matter of public policy to prevent the deterioration of land.
Question	You agree to cultivate Thompson's land on shares. Before the cultivation of the crop is completed, you abandon the land without justification. Are you still entitled to your share of the crops?
Answer	No. The landlord is entitled to take the whole crop; you would also be liable in damages for breach of contract to cultivate. However, you do not lose your right to a share of the crop by abandoning the cultivation of the land. You are justified in doing so, for example, when the behavior of the landlord provokes you into leaving.
Question	You enter into a written agreement to rent an apartment at $50 per month for a period of one year. You give the prospective landlord a deposit as evidence of your good faith, obtaining a receipt. Your family, living in another city, is brought to town, sending on the furniture by express. The day before you are to move in, the landlord notifies you that he has rented the apartment to someone else. What can you do?
Answer	You can sue the landlord for breach of contract. You may

recover, usually, damages which are the natural, direct and necessary consequence of the landlord's failure to give you possession of the apartment; specifically, you may recover the expense you and your family have been put to—railroad fare, shipping charges for household furniture and belongings, etc. You may not, however, recover for the inconvenience to which you and your family have been put.

Question   You obtain a cigar concession in a hotel. A few months after you acquire possession, the hotel is forced to close for lack of business. What are your rights?

Answer   You have a claim against the landlord for damages.

Question   After renting you a house, your landlord acts disagreeably to you, makes all sorts of insulting remarks, threatens to forcibly dispossess you and finally advertises the house for rent. What are your rights?

Answer   You may rightfully abandon the house, refuse to pay rent and file suit against the landlord for damages.

Question   A tenant leases an apple orchard but fails to take care of it properly. May the owner cancel the lease?

Answer   Yes. This is permitted so that further waste and destruction may be prevented.

Advisory 8

PARTNERSHIP

There are three ways, generally, in which a business enterprise may be carried on. The first is where the business is owned solely by one man, the proprietor, who retains all the profits for himself and is alone responsible for the firm's debts and obligations. Most small concerns are still conducted in this fashion, occasionally even some very large ones.

A second type of legal organization is the partnership. A partnership represents a division of responsibility and profits. It often happens, for example, that one individual, unable by himself to raise the requisite capital, is forced to seek an association with others whose wealth, combined with his own, fulfills the needs of the enterprise. On the other hand, one prospective partner may have money to invest but not sufficient experience to make a go of the venture, while the other prospective partner possesses experience but lacks capital. By combining the two and forming a partnership, a solution is provided.

Forming a partnership, then, has practical advantages; but it is fraught with dangers, too. By its very nature, a partnership is a highly personal relationship which should not be entered into lightly or without careful investigation of the character and financial background of the proposed members. For partners not only share in the profits, but in the losses as well. As we shall see, one partner has the inherent power to bind other members within the partnership. Moreover, the personal assets of each partner may be seized by creditors of the firm to pay off partnership obligations; or, to take another example, the assets of one member may be taken to pay all the theft or defalcation of dishonest members.

Question   What is a partnership?

Answer   A partnership is an association of two or more persons to carry on, as co-owners, a business for profit. It is less formally organized than a corporation, and burdens of taxation and the tiling of returns and statements are much lighter. Unlike a stockholder in a corporation, a partner is subject to personal liability for the obligations of the partnership; he is also subject to liability for any loss due to the incompetence or fraud of his associates.

Question   What are some of the rights and obligations of a partnership?

Answer   The acts of each partner are the acts of all partners; each partner is agent for the firm and for the other partners; all are liable, as partners, upon contracts made by any of them with third persons within the scope of the partnership business; not only is the partnership property liable for debts incurred by the partnership, but the individual property of each partner is also liable, each partner being individually liable for the acts of the partnership.

Question   What is the extent of a partner's liability?

Answer   A partner is liable for all debts regularly contracted by the firm.

Question   What is the difference between a limited and unlimited partnership?

Answer   The difference is the extent to which partners may be liable. In the usual or unlimited partnership, the partners are liable to creditors for firm debts, since, in partnership law, they are individual debts. Limited partnerships are organized to permit all or some members to limit their liability to creditors to the amount of their subscription to the capital stock.

Question   What is the difference between a general and special partner?

Answer   A general partner has ownership of the partnership property, or a share in such property, full powers of management within the partnership purposes and full personal liability. A special partner is an investor who receives a share of the property or profits, but has no powers of management and no personal liability beyond the amount of his investment.

Question   What is an ostensible partner?

Answer   He is a person who, though not actually a partner, represents himself as being one, or consents to being so represented by those who carry on the business. As far as third persons are concerned, who act on such representations, an ostensible partner is subject to liability as if he were an actual partner.

Question   What is a dormant or silent partner?

Answer   Such a partner is one whose name is not used and who is, so inactive in the partnership that his relationship to it is generally unknown. A dormant or silent partner, however, is liable for all partnership obligations while a member of the partnership.

Question   What is an incoming partner and what is the extent of his liability?

Answer   An incoming partner is one brought into a going business as a new partner. He is not personally liable on old obligations, unless he actually answers them. He is liable, however, for his capital contribution in the partnership property.

Question   What is a retiring partner?

Answer   He is one who, after a partnership is dissolved, ceases to be a partner in the business which is carried on by others. He remains liable for partnership obligations incurred while he was a partner, but is not liable for new obligations unless he fails to give the necessary notice of withdrawal. Those, who continue a business after dissolution are called continuing partners.

Question   What is a surviving partner?

Answer   He is one who remains after the dissolution of the partnership or death of a partner or partners. A surviving partner succeeds to the ownership of the partnership property and is charged with the duty of liquidation unless, by agreement, the business is to be continued.

Question   What constitutes firm property?

Answer   Whatever is contributed to the firm by any partner, or is acquired by it, is firm property.

Question   What should the partnership agreement (or Articles of Partnership) contain?

Answer   It should contain the names of the partners; the name of the partnership; the nature of the business to be conducted; when the partnership is to begin and how long it is to continue; the place where the partnership is to be carried on; the share each partner is to contribute, and the form in which it shall be contributed by him and at What time; the interest each partner shall have in the partnership (otherwise the interests are presumed to be equal, notwithstanding the fact that the contributions may be unequal); the liability for losses to be borne by each partner; the duties of each partner; when accountings shall be made between' the partners; how much each partner shall be. entitled to draw; how partnership books are to be kept; whether any partner is to draw a salary and, if so, the amount; how the partnership may be dissolved, the disposition of the good will and property and finally, how disputes between the partners are to be settled.

Question   Must a partnership agreement be in writing?

Answer   No, but it is more desirable and affords greater protection to all parties if it is.

Question   May a person under legal age be a partner?

Answer   Yes. However, an infant incurs no liability and is not responsible for the debts of the firm during his infancy. When an infant comes of age, he may, if he wishes, affirm past transactions which will make him liable.

Question   John, age twenty, is a member of a partnership; he is known as such by persons dealing with the firm. Upon reaching twenty-one, John neither affirms nor disaffirms the partnership. Creditors now seek to hold John liable for the debts of the partnership. May they?

Answer   Yes. A person who, before coming of age, represents himself to be a partner must, when he reaches his majority, notify creditors that he has ceased to be a partner if he wishes to avoid liability.

Question   Jones, Smith and Thompson form a partnership, Jones contributing $ 5,000, Smith $3,000 and Thompson his time and skill. In the absence of any express provision in the agreement, what share of the profits are the three entitled to?

Answer   They are entitled to share equally in the profits. Upon dissolution, Jones and Smith are entitled to recover their contributions first, before Thompson receives his share.

Question   Smith 8: Company owns an automobile. What interest does Jones, a partner, have in the vehicle?

Answer   The automobile is held as a "tenancy in partnership." This means that each partner has the right, with his col partners, to the possession of the partnership property for partnership purposes. Neither partner, however, has the right to possess the automobile for any other purpose, without the consent of the other partner. On the death of one partner, his right to specific partnership property (the car, in this case) passes to the surviving partners. When the deceased is the last surviving partner, the partnership property passes to his executor or administrator. A partner cannot assign, transfer or sell partnership property except by and with the consent of all the partners.

Question Arnold, owner of a zinc mine, enters into a written agreement with Bertelli, by which he agrees to furnish Bertelli a certain quantity of ore annually, for three years, on being paid $10 per ton. Bertelli agrees to provide suitable buildings and machinery for the ore's conversion into paints, etc., and to divide with Arnold the profits of the enterprise, one-fourth to himself and the balance to Arnold. The cost of the buildings and machinery is to be paid out of the profits, after a specified time. Creditors of Arnold now seek to hold the assets of Bertelli on the theory that Arnold and Bertelli are partners. Can they?

Answer Yes. In this example, Arnold and Bertelli are partners— each would be liable for partnership debts. There are both a community of interest and a sharing of profits. When you have this, you have a partnership.

Question Lewis buys a half-interest in a manufacturing plant for $10,000, agreeing to hire a manager at his own expense. Lewis agrees to pay the manager $100 per month, as well as one-fourth of the net profits. It is also provided that the firm, if dissatisfied, may end the employment by notice, upon which the manager's future interest in the business or under the contract would cease. The manager is discharged on notice. There are no net profits. After his discharge, the manager seeks to have Lewis give an accounting, on the theory that he is a partner and hence entitled to one. Is he right?

Answer No. This arrangement is not a partnership, the payment of a share of the profits being merely incidental to the employment contract. As an employee, the manager is not entitled to an accounting which he could secure through the courts were he a partner.

Question Jones owns a store building. Smith offers to rent it from Jones proposing that Jones shall have one-third of the net profits of the business so rented. Are Jones and Smith partners in this enterprise, making Jones liable for Smith's losses or debts?

Answer	No. Here, there is no intention to create a co-ownership in the business. In addition to a sharing in net profits by the participants in a business enterprise, they must intend to be co-owners of the business.
Question	An owner of a factory employs a manager to take charge, the manager to receive one-fourth of the net profits as his compensation. There is no understanding that the manager is to be a co-owner. When the factory becomes insolvent (unable to pay its debts), creditors seek to hold the assets of the manager on the theory that he is a partner. Can they?
Answer	No. The manager is simply an employee, not a partner, and as such is not liable to creditors for losses, nor must he share losses with the owner.
Question	A literary society is organized for cultural purposes in which you become a member. The society, in the course of time, acquires $4,000. Soon thereafter, you allege that the funds have been misapplied and seek to have the club dissolved. You also seek to obtain an accounting of its funds, although the by-laws of the organization forbid a dissolution while ten members remain, unless by unanimous consent. Will you succeed?
Answer	No. The society is not a partnership, since it is not run for profit. The money acquired by the organization is merely incidental to its main purpose, which is literary.
Question	An insolvent partnership agrees with creditors that the business shall be continued under the supervision of a managing committee, designated by the creditors, until their claims are fully paid out of the profits. Are the creditors, who are parties to this agreement, liable as partners to the new creditors of the business?
Answer	No. They are not co-owners of the business, since it is not carried on primarily for the creditors' benefit; hence, the creditors' interest in the property and in the profits is limited to the definite amount of their claims.
Question	What powers does a partner have?
Answer	One of the most important is the power to bind the firm in the usual operation of the business it carries on. A partner also has apparent authority to replenish the stock in trade, buy and sell stock in the course of business and make contracts in reference to it.
Question	Two partners are in the radio business. One of them buys

radios on the credit of the firm. He then pawns the radios for his own use. Is the other partner bound on the purchase?

Answer   Yes. Every partner has the power to buy and sell stock in trade. It is immaterial whether the partner deflects from its proper use goods bought by him for the firm.

Question   Smith and Jones are partners in a dairy business. Smith sells one of the cows without Jones' consent. May Jones recover the cow from the purchaser?

Answer   Yes. A sale of capital assets with which the concern carries on its business (in this case, a cow) is not binding unless actually authorized or ratified by the other partners.

Question   Has a partner power to buy or sell real estate?

Answer   No, unless he is expressly authorized to do so.

Question   Smith and Jones are in the package liquor business. Smith borrows money from Cornwall, ostensibly on account of the firm and for fun purposes. He gives a note in the firm's name for its repayment. Actually, Jones never authorized the loan, received no benefit from it, nor did he affirm it. Cornwell now wants to hold Smith and Jones as partners, under Smith's apparent authority to bind the firm. May he do so?

Answer   Yes. If negotiable paper is issued, accepted or indorsed by a partner whose business requires the use of negotiable paper the firm is liable. Hence, if one partner signs the names of all the partners, or the partnership name, all the partners are bound, provided the first partner had apparent authority to sign.

Question   Three men are partners in the sale of stock. One of the partners sells stock in a corporation to Jones, guaranteeing payment in a writing signed by the partnership name. The corporation in which the stock is held becomes insolvent, and Jones now seeks to hold all the partners liable on the guaranty. Actually, two of the partners never consented to or ratified the act of the third partner. May they be held?

Answer   Yes; A partner may make ordinary warranties or representations which will be binding on all the partners.

Question   Jones and Smith are partners in a grocery store. Reed, who owes the firm money, pays his bill to Jones who absconds. May Smith compel Reed to pay him again?

Answer   No. Payment to one partner is payment to the partnerships.

Question   Robinson, a partner in a firm, buys shares in a mining

	company in his own name without the authority of the other partners, but with the money and on account of the firm. Who is entitled to the shares, Robinson or the firm?
Answer	The firm. It is presumed, unless a contrary intention appears, that property acquired with partnership funds is partnership property.
Question	A package liquor store, operated by three partners, gives a note signed merely by the hurt name. Are all three partners bound on the note?
Answer	Yes. A partnership name is the name of all the partners. The use of that name, with the authority of the firm, binds all the members, even though one partner does not sign the note.
Question	A partnership firm desires to purchase real estate. Should title he acquired in the firm name, or in the names of all the members?
Answer	Title should be taken in the names of all the members, or one of them in trust for the others. This must be done because title to real estate is a matter of record and must be lodged either in a natural person, or persons, or in a corporation.
Question	Jones, Smith, Roberts and Reed are partners in a sugar refinery business. Roberts is the managing partner, also doing business separately, with the consent of the others, as a sugar dealer. He buys sugar in his separate business, selling it to the firm at a profit without letting the other partners know that the sugar is his. Is the firm entitled to Roberts' profits on such sales?
Answer	Yes. Each partner must account to the firm for any benefit derived by him, without the consent of the other partners, from any transaction involving the partnership.
Question	A firm is anxious to purchase some motor trucks. Jones, a partner, owns some trucks which are titled in another's name. Without revealing this fact, he induces his partner, Smith, to buy the vehicles. Upon discovering the facts, Smith wishes to cancel the transaction. May he?
Answer	Yes. A partner must not turn partnership advantages to himself, or in any way oppose his interests to those of the arm, unless there is consent and a full disclosure of all the important facts.
Question	Jones, Smith and Thompson form a partnership, each contributing $5,000. It is understood that all shall be

equally active in conducting the firm's affairs. The partnership lasts for a year. During that time, Jones goes to Europe for three months and Smith suffers poor health, remaining at home most of that time. Thompson puts in long hours to help keep the business going successfully. Upon dissolution, Thompson claims a right to a salary for the time when he alone kept the business going. Is he entitled to it?

Answer No. Each partner engages in the business for the profits to be made therein. Hence, no partner is entitled to extra compensation for services unless there is a specific agreement to this effect. This applies even where the duties of one partner are unusually burdensome, due to the neglect of the other partners.

Question Jones and Smith are partners in an established business when Thompson is taken into the firm. At that time, Reed is a creditor of Jones and Smith. Is Thompson, by his entrance into the partnership, obligated also to Reed?

Answer Yes, but his liability can be satisfied only out of partnership property, not his individual property.

Question After Smith's death, surviving partners in Smith, Jones and Company continue under the same name, arranging with Charles Smith, brother of the deceased John Smith, for the use of his name, although Charles Smith does not become a partner. Creditors of the firm now seek to hold Smith liable as a partner. May they?

Answer Yes. Charles Smith is a partner by "estoppel." This occurs when a person, by words or by conduct, represents himself, or permits another to represent him, as a partner in an existing partnership. Such a partner is liable to any such person to whom such representations have been made and who, has, on the faith of such representation, extended credit. In the above illustration, creditors continued doing business with the firm, aware that Smith's name was used. Knowing this, Smith failed to repudiate the action. Charles Smith, therefore, is liable to every person dealing with the firm—precisely as though he were an actual partner.

Question How may a partnership be dissolved?

Answer
1. When the time stipulated in the agreement expires.
2. By mutual consent.
3. By transfer of a partner's interest.
4. By death of a partner.
5. By bankruptcy.

6. By judicial decree because of (a) internal dissension, (b) a partner's incapacity, (c) a partner's misconduct or, finally, (d) the financial failure of the business.

Question   John, Bill and Henry form a partnership. Shortly afterward, John retires from the business. Are Bill and Henry still partners?

Answer   No. Retirement of a partner automatically dissolves a partnership, unless the enterprise is continued by the remaining partners in accordance with the Articles of Partnership or with the consent of all members. This is true, also, where a partner dies or becomes insane.

Question   Smith operates a hardware store. His son joins him in the business, under an agreement whereby he is to have one-half of the profits. The business is conducted under the name of "Smith and Son." A few years later, the son withdraws from the firm which is continued by the father under the old name, with the son's knowledge. Jones sells goods to the store, seeking to hold the son as a partner. May he?

Answer   Yes. A person may be held liable as a partner because of his failure to notify others that the partnership is dissolved.

Question   Smith, Jones and Reed are partners. Jones withdraws. What should he do to protect himself against future liability as a member of that firm?

Answer   Upon withdrawing, a partner should notify all those who may continue to deal with the firm in the belief that he is still a partner. Otherwise, he may be liable for the firm's indebtedness even after his withdrawal. He should give actual notice to all who have dealt with the him. To all others, it suffices if he publishes notice of his withdrawal in a newspaper.

Question   Jones and Smith enter into Articles of Partnership for two years. After one year, Jones forcibly excludes Smith from the partnership place of business, refusing to permit him to further participate in firm affairs. Jones also refuses to pay Smith any share of profits or to make any division of partnership property. What can Smith do?

Answer   He can sue for damages, his damages being the value of the partnership interest. He may also go into court to have the partnership dissolved, and ask for an accounting, as well as damages for breach of contract.

Question   Jones and Smith, having been partners, dissolve the firm.

	Jones taking over the business and property. Jones gives Reed several notes in the name of the old partnership. Is Smith bound by the notes?
Answer	No. Unless Smith has expressly authorized the continued use of the old name of the firm for that purpose, he would not be bound.
Question	Jones and Smith are partners. The partnership is dissolved by consent; it is agreed that the assets and business of the firm shall be sold at auction. Jones, nevertheless, continues to carry on the business on the partnership premises, with the partnership property and capital. Must Jones account to Smith for the profits thus made?
Answer	Yes. Where any member of a firm dies or otherwise ceases to be a partner, and the surviving or continuing partners carry on the business without any final settlement of accounts as between the firm and the outgoing partner, then, in the absence of any agreement to the contrary, the outgoing partner or his estate is entitled to such share of the profits made since the dissolution.
Question	A clause in a partnership agreement between Smith and Jones provides that, upon the death of either partner, the survivor shall purchase his share at a fixed value. Smith and Jones continue their business in partnership after the expiration of the term, which is two years. Subsequently, Smith dies and Jones now seeks to buy Smith's share at the fixed value set in the original partnership agreement. May he do so?
Answer	Yes. Where a partnership is entered into for a fixed term and is continued after its expiration without any express new agreement, the rights, and duties of the partners remain the same as they were at the expiration of the term.
Question	Jones, Smith and Reed are partners. By consent, Reed withdraws from the firm, leaving Jones and Smith. Is Reed still liable for the debts incurred while a member of the firm?
Answer	Yes. He cannot, by withdrawing, deprive creditors of their rights against him, even though he has an agreement with the remaining partners whereby they assume the existing indebtedness.

Advisory 9

CORPORATIONS

The third and final basic type of business organization is the corporation. In the preceding chapter, we saw that a partnership entailed a division of profits and losses, each partner being personally liable for the firm's debts and obligations. It was to escape this Onerous burden of liability that the corporation was devised for, unlike a partnership, liability of shareholders in a corporation is limited to the amount of their subscriptions.

A corporation, moreover, has a personality distinct from its stockholders, having rights and duties apart from its members. A corporation, for example, may own an office building but the individual members have no rights therein again, a corporation may owe money but the shareholders re under no obligation to pay the debt.

In a partnership, you will recall, the firm is dissolved upon the death of any of its members. A corporation, on the other hand, enjoys perpetual succession and may continue in existence long after the death of the original line operators. It is this fact of perpetual succession which listing distinguishes a corporation from all other types of business organization, giving it the considerable advantage it enjoys increasingly, the corporation has become the form in which business is organized.

Question	What is a corporation?
Answer	A corporation is a body, consisting of one or more natural persons, established by law, usually for some specific purpose, continued by a succession of members.
Question	What are some of the characteristics of a corporation?
Answer	1. To have continuous succession, without being subject to dissolution by the death, withdrawal or legal disability of any of its individual members.

2. To take and grant property and contract obligations, within the limits of its charter.

3. To sue and be sued in its corporate name, in the same manner as an individual.

4. To receive grants of privileges and immunities.

5. Exemption of its members from personal liability for the debts of the corporation beyond the amount of their respective shares.

6. To buy and sell real estate.

7. Power to use a common seal.

8. Power to make by-laws.

9. Power to transfer membership in the corporation without the consent of the other members.

Question   What are the advantages in forming a corporation?

Answer   One of the most important advantages is that liability of shareholders is limited to the amount of their subscriptions. Once the shareholder has paid the par value of his stock, he is no longer liable either to the corporation itself or to creditors of the corporation. In a partnership, the liability is personal and unlimited. Creditors, for example, may, out of the assets of any single partner, collect their judgments, something which cannot occur in a corporation. Another advantage is that members of a corporation are not liable for the unauthorized acts of their associates. If anyone is liable, it is the corporation itself. Again, the corporate form has a permanency afforded by no other type of business organization. When a partner or the owner of a business dies, a reorganization is necessary if the business is to continue. The death of any officer or member does not dissolve the corporation, however. Finally, the formation of a corporation often is a greater inducement than a partnership for raising capital and borrowing money. In this way, corporation shares can be more readily sold than shares in a similar but unincorporated business.

Question   Are there any reasons for not incorporating?

Answer   The main one is that a corporation is burdened by excessive taxation and franchise licenses to carry on the corporate business.

Question   What is an eleemosynary corporation?

Answer   Such a corporation is formed to distribute the bounty of the founder in such manner as he has directed. It includes hospitals for the relief of the poor and the weak, colleges for the promotion of learning, and the support of persons engaged in literary pursuits. It is generally synonymous with a charitable organization.

Question   What is a corporation sole?

Answer   It is a corporation which, by law, consists of but one member at any one time—as a bishop in England for example.

Question   What is a foreign corporation?

Answer   This is a corporation created by legislation other than the one in which its right to do business or own property is being considered. For example, a corporation created under the law of New York is a foreign corporation in Maryland.

Question   What is a nonprofit corporation?

Answer   This is a corporation having no capital stock and not being operated for financial profit. Lodges, pleasure clubs, church organizations, etc., are examples.

Question   Are non-profit or charitable corporations liable for the negligence of their employees?

Answer   No, not when the person suing is a beneficiary of the charity. A charitable corporation is generally held liable to strangers for the negligence of its employees within the scope of their employment.

Question   What should be considered in determining the state of incorporation?

Answer   In general, a corporation should be organized in the state in which its principal business is to be conducted, unless certain advantages and privileges are needed which can be acquired only under the laws of another state. Some of the most important matters to be considered are:

1. Fees and taxes.
2. Requirements as to the issue of shares.
3. Convenience of operation, such as requirements as to qualifications and residence of directors, etc.
4 Ease of making corporate changes.
5. Limitations on the power of corporations to declare dividends and the purchase of its own shares and shares of other corporations.
6. Liabilities imposed by statute on directors and shareholders for debts of the corporation, etc.
7. Right to remove cases to the federal courts.

Question How is an ordinary business corporation organized?

Answer 1. By having a lawyer draft the Articles of Incorporation.

2. By having the corporation papers signed by the requisite number of incorporators and the acknowledgment of their signatures before a Notary Public.

3. By filing or recording the Articles or Certificate with the Secretary of State and payment of the organization fees.

4. By filing or recording a certified copy of the Articles or Certificate with the county clerk in which the principal office is located.

5. By electing directors and holding an organization meeting by the shareholders and directors.

6. By procuring a permit or license to do business.

7. By complying with the Federal Securities Act.

Question What takes place at the first corporate meeting?

Answer Generally, stock subscribers come together and elect the Board of Directors. By-laws are adopted or a committee is appointed to draw them up. After their election, the directors elect officers of the corporation and perform such other business as may be properly presented, such as propositions to exchange property or services for stock.

Question What are the by-laws of a corporation?

Answer These are rules passed for the internal government of the corporation. They are alterable at its pleasure and are binding on the stockholders so long as they are regularly enacted. They must not be contrary to the law or the charter of the corporation, or against public policy.

Question With what do by-laws deal?

Answer They are usually concerned with the duties and qualifications of directors and officers; terms of office; bonds of officers; dates of regular meetings; and how special meetings may be called.

Question Who determines the by-laws of a corporation?

Answer Usually the stockholders, unless, by statute, power is delegated to the directors.

Question What should the Articles or Certificate of Incorporation contain?

Answer 1. The name of the corporation, which must not be in conflict with an existing name.

2. The purposes for which it is formed.

3. The authorized capital structure, i.e., the number of shares and whether or not they shall have a par value, the different classes of shares, common or preferred, and the preferences and restrictions thereof.

4. The principal place of business or office. The period of time for which the corporation is organized.

5. The number of directors, usually not less than three, with their names and addresses.
6. The names and addresses of the incorporators.

7. The amount of subscribed and paid-in capital with which the corporation proposes to do business.

8. The amount of indebtedness authorized, and limitation, if any, of stockholder's liability.

9. The execution and acknowledgment.

Question	What is the charter of a corporation?
Answer	A charter is the contract between the state and the corporation and defines its powers. A corporation has only those powers expressly contained in its charter, as well as those reasonably necessary to carry them out.
Question	What should be contained in a corporate charter?
Answer	1. The name of the proposed corporation.
	2. The objects of the corporation.
	3. The amount of capital stock.
	4. The number and amount of shares.
	5. The classes of stock.
	6. The duration of life of the corporation.
	7. The location of the principal office.
Question	Who issues the corporate charter?
Answer	The state.
Question	A corporate charter is granted by the State of South Carolina. The corporators, who are authorized to act as directors until others shall be elected, assemble in Baltimore, pass resolutions of acceptance and perform other acts necessary to organize the corporation. Has the corporation legal existence?
Answer	No. A corporation can have no legal existence outside the

boundaries of the state by which it is created. To be effective, acceptance of the charter and organization under it must take place within the State of South Carolina. Since they took place in Maryland, the corporate proceedings are void.

Question   Under a charter granted by the State of Maine, the corporators meet in New York, where. they organize and accept the charter, electing officers and directors. The directors then meet in New York and authorize the president and secretary to execute a mortgage on the corporate property, which is done. Is this a good mortgage?

Answer   No. The action of the corporators in meeting and electing officers is a corporate act which could not take place outside the state of incorporation. Hence, the directors being illegally chosen, the mortgage is void.

Question   A state law requires, as a preliminary to incorporation, that articles be filed with the Clerk of the Court of Appeals and a duplicate with the Clerk of the judicial district. The duplicate is not filed as required. Nevertheless, the business functions under the corporate name. Creditors of the corporation file suit against it. Can they recover against the corporation?

Answer   No. Since the corporation lacked a charter and failed to comply with the statutory requirements, no corporation legally existed. Hence, the indebtedness is a personal one, not a corporate obligation.

Question   A subscriber to stock in a corporation to be formed takes an active part in its organization, as well as in its management after organization. When the corporation files suit against him for his unpaid subscription, he defends on the ground that the corporation was not legally organized. Is this a good defense?

Answer   No. A person who undertakes to form a corporation, later participating in its management, cannot dispute the existence of the corporation, nor can he avoid liability on his stock subscription in the pretended corporation when sued thereon, either by it or its creditors.

Question   A state law requires that the charter give the names of the incorporators. A charter is procured, however, which fails to provide such information. Has a valid corporation been formed?

Answer   Yes. A corporation, defectively organized, may still have progressed to a point to give the company sufficient legal standing, as a corporate body, for it to transact business and incur liabilities. Compliance with the law has gone far enough, in this example, to enable the company to function as a corporation. Its members, therefore, would not personally be liable, only the corporation itself.

Question Jackson contracts with an association of persons, becoming their creditor. He does so without any knowledge that they claim to be a corporation instead of partners, and there is nothing to put him on notice. As a matter of fact, the group of persons had organized themselves defectively as a corporation. Jackson now seeks to hold them as partners, there being no corporate assets. May he do so?

Answer Yes. Jackson may sue the members as partners, showing that they failed to comply with the law under which they claim corporate existence.

Question May a corporation adopt any name it pleases?

Answer Yes, as long as its name does not conflict with that of an existing concern. A corporation adopting a name already in use, for the purpose of attracting the other's business, may be restrained by injunction or be liable in damages.

Question How is membership acquired in a corporation?

Answer In non-stock corporations, membership is regulated by the charter and by-laws. Membership in stock corporations is determined by the ownership of one or more shares of the capital stock secured either (1) by subscription to the capital stock, before or after incorporation, (2) by purchase from the corporation, (3) by transfer from the owner.

Question What books should a corporation keep?

Answer 1. Books which are regularly kept in any business.

2. Special corporate books which include the minute book, containing the minutes of the corporation; the stock certificate book, consisting of a number of blank stock certificates in the form authorized by the directors, numbered consecutively, attached to "stubs" containing corresponding serial numbers. When required, these certificates are detached from the stubs and tilled in, with the stockholder's name and the number of shares it represents, the stub being a record of the transaction. 7726 stock ledger, showing the status of each shareholder

in relation to the company It contains the name of each recorded stockholder, alphabetically arranged, his address, the number of shares owned by him, the date and source of the transaction, the date of the disposition. of any shares and to whom disposed, and how much stock remains in his credit; the transfer book, consisting of a series of blank transfer forms to be tilled out and signed by the transferor or his agent; a corporate calendar, kept by the secretary, covering the entire year and indicating to him the days on which notices are to be sent, meetings held, taxes payable, when reports to state officers are due, etc.

Question Has a stockholder a right to examine books of the corporation?

Answer Yes. A stockholder has a right to inspect the books and papers of a corporation, either personally or by an agent, provided he does so for a proper purpose and at a proper time. Thus, a stockholder showing a prima facie case of fraud, and whose purpose is to obtain information to remedy the fraud, is entitled to inspect corporate books and papers. A stockholder has no right of inspection, however, where his purpose in making the examination is improper, or hostile to the interests of the corporation, or merely frivolous.

Question What is meant by the capital stock of a corporation?

Answer This is the amount of money or property subscribed and paid in by the shareholders or authorized to be so paid in. It always remains the same, unless changed by law. The capital stock of a corporation does not necessarily indicate the value of the property of the company.

Question Of what does the capital of a corporation consist?

Answer The capital of a corporation consists of its funds, securities, credits and property of any kind, owned by the corporation.

Question What is authorized capital stock?

Answer This is the amount of stock a corporation is authorized to issue under its charter. The issued stock is that actually is sued within the authorized limit.

Question What does a share of stock represent?

Answer A share of stock is the right, to partake in the surplus profits of a corporation; and, upon the dissolution of the corporation, to partake of the fund representing the capital stock as is not liable for the debts of the corporation.

Question   What is a stock certificate?

Answer   It is a written acknowledgment by the corporation of the interest of the holder in its property and franchises.

Question   What is meant by a stock subscription?

Answer   A subscription to the stock of an existing corporation, when accepted, is a contract between the subscriber and the corporation. It is subject to the rules governing other kinds of contracts.

Question   What is the usual method of subscribing to stock in a corporation not yet formed?

Answer   Generally, the procedure is for the parties to sign an agreement to form the corporation and take stock in it when organized.

Question   A railroad company is organized under a law which appoints commissioners to open books and receive stock subscriptions. Jackson subscribes to some stock; his name being properly recorded in the books. Shortly afterwards, having changed his mind, Jackson attempts to withdraw his subscription. May he do so?

Answer   No. Jackson's subscription is an offer on his part to purchase stock on the terms set forth by the corporation. When that offer is accepted by the corporation, in this case the railroad company, a binding contract results, and neither party may then withdraw from the agreement. The corporation's acceptance is indicated by having Jackson's subscription recorded in its books.

Question   A subscription to stock in a railroad company provides that one-fourth shall be paid when the road is completed to a certain county line, the remainder to be paid in four equal monthly installments, provided the company establishes a depot on said road at a certain point. The road is completed to the specified county line, but there is no erection of the depot. Because of this, the subscriber seeks to cancel his subscription. May he do so?

Answer   No. The completion of the road to the specified county line is a condition precedent to any liability on the subscription, being made so by the subscription agreement. The erection of the depot is an independent stipulation, not a condition precedent to liability on the subscription. Whether a particular stipulation is a condition precedent, or merely an independent stipulation, is a question of intention, courts taking into consideration not only the words of the particular clause, but also the language of the entire contract, the situation of the parties, the nature of the act required and the whole subject matter to which it relates.

Question What is treasury stock?

Answer This is issued stock re-acquired by the corporation and held in its treasury for possible reissuance.

Question What is the difference between common and preferred stock?

Answer Preferred stock, usually, entitles the holder to preference over the holder of common stock, both in 'the participation of earnings and in the division of assets. Being stockholders, the owners of preferred shares are subject to all the liabilities of stockholders, including liability for corporate debts.

Question What is "participating" preferred stock?

Answer Such stock not only entitles the holder to the preferences described in Question 40, but also participates with the common stock in the earnings above the percent agreed upon. For example, if there is a seven per cent participating preferred stock, it must he paid seven per cent before anything is paid on the common stock.

Question What is meant by "watered" stock?

Answer This is stock issued gratuitously, or under an agreement by which the holder is to pay less than its par value, either in money, property or services. Watered stock issued by a corporation is binding on it, and also binds stockholders who participate or acquiesce in the transaction. Dissenting stockholders, however, may sue to enjoin or cancel the issue of such stock. Again, if the watered stock is original stock, issued on subscription, the transaction is a fraud on creditors of the corporation, who deal with it on the faith of the stock being fully paid. Hence, if the corporation becomes insolvent, the original holders of such stock, and purchasers with notice, may be held liable for its par value to pay such creditors.

Question It is agreed between a corporation and all its stockholders that only twenty-five per cent should be paid on their shares. Subsequently, the corporation seeks to collect the full value of its stock. May it do so?

Answer No. This is a perfectly valid agreement; it is as binding as between the company and its stockholders, as if it were expressly authorized by charter. No suit, therefore, can be maintained by the corporation to collect the unpaid stock, since the shares were issued as fully paid and on a fair understanding.

Question   What is a "blue sky" law?

Answer   Such laws are designed to prevent the sale of stock, the only assets of which are "blue sky." They provide for the registration of the proposed stock with the proper body, with the provision that the securities are not to be issued until so registered and passed upon, and a license to sell is granted by the Federal Securities Commission. The effect of such laws, where properly enforced, is to regulate the sale of speculative securities, though it does not actually forbid them.

Question   What does the Federal Securities Law provide?

Answer   This act, passed by Congress in 1933, provides for full disclosure of facts concerning securities offered in interstate commerce or through the mails. Under the act, a registration must be filed with the Securities and Exchange Commission in Washington by the registrant, including financial statements, pertinent exhibits and a copy of the "prospectus." The law prescribes certain penalties for failure to file a full and honest report.

Question   What is a dividend?

Answer   A dividend is a fund which the corporation has set apart from its profits to be divided among its members.

Question   Who declares dividends?

Answer   The directors of a corporation. They have large discretionary powers, and are therefore not accountable unless they abuse this discretion and act fraudulently, oppressively or unreasonably.

Question   Who are entitled to dividends?

Answer   Stockholders of record at the time the dividend is declared, no matter when the profits were earned, and without regard to the length of time particular members may have been stockholders.

Question   May a stockholder bring suit against the corporation to compel it to declare dividends where there is a surplus?

Answer   No. He can only bring suit after the dividend has been declared, for, until that time, no dividend is due. However, should the directors fraudulently fail to declare a dividend or act in obvious bad faith, stockholders may go into a court of equity to compel the directors to declare a dividend. A stockholder may obtain an injunction, if he can secure no other relief, restraining or preventing the directors or other officers of the corporation from paying out money on purposes thought to be illegal.

Question May a dividend be declared where there are no profits or surplus?

Answer No, to do so is improper.

Question An insolvent corporation declares a dividend. May creditors of the corporation recover such dividend?

Answer Yes. Creditors may recover from each stockholder who has been paid a dividend, such dividend being considered a fraud on creditors of the corporation.

Question A dividend is declared in June, payable in August. In July, a stockholder transfers his stock to Bill. Is Bill entitled to the dividend?

Answer No.

Question A corporation declares a dividend, paying it to those stockholders who are registered as such on the books of the corporation. Jones, a former stockholder, has sold and assigned his stock to Collins before the declaration of the dividend, but the latter has not yet had the stock transferred to his name. As between Jones and Collins, who is entitled to the dividend?

Answer Collins. The rule is that a dividend is payable to the substantial owner of the shares at the time the dividend is declared.

Question What constitutes a legal meeting of stockholders, so as to render the acts and vote of the majority binding?

Answer 1. The meeting must be called by one having authority. In the absence of provision to the contrary, such authority exists in the directors or managing agents.

2. Notice of time and place of the meeting must be given to each stockholder, unless the time and place are definitely fixed by statute, charter, by-laws or usage. But if all the stockholders are present, in person or by proxy, notice is waived.

3. If a special meeting is called, notice of the business to be transacted must be given.

4. The meeting must be held at a reasonable time and place.

5. It must be regularly and properly conducted.

6. If there is a provision that a certain number of stock. holders shall constitute a quorum for the transaction of business, a less number cannot act. In the absence of express provision, no particular number is necessary to constitute a quorum.

Question   May a stockholder be prevented from attending a stockholders' meeting?

Answer   No.

Question   Who are entitled to vote?

Answer   Those who appear on the books of the corporation as its stockholders.

Question   If a stockholder cannot attend a meeting, does he lose his right to vote?

Answer   No. He may vote by "proxy"—that is, by sending someone to attend the meeting in his place and to vote in his stead.

Question   Do trustees, executors and administrators have the right to vote?

Answer   Yes. They may vote the stock they hold in trust.

Question   In general, what are the powers of majority stockholders?

Answer   As a rule, each shareholder is bound by all acts and proceedings, within the scope of the powers and authority can ferred by the charter, which are adopted by a vote of the majority of the corporation, duly taken in accordance with the law. However, if the charter grants the board of directors, or other agents with power to manage the corporate affairs, the power is exclusive and cannot be controlled or interfered with by the stockholders, their remedy being to elect or an point new directors or agents. At the same time, even the majority cannot bind the minority by acts beyond the corporation's authority, nor defeat or impair contract rights between the corporation and individual stockholders, nor act fraudulently or oppressively, as against the minority.

Question   In violation of its charter, a majority of stockholders in a corporation sell, at a loss, several buildings belonging to the corporation. Is such a transaction binding on the corporation?

Answer   No. Even a majority of stockholders have no power to bind the minority by any act or proceeding not within the powers conferred upon the corporation by its charter. In this case, a stockholder, on behalf of himself and other stockholders, may bring suit against the corporation in a court of equity. As a basis for the suit it must be shown; (1) that some action, or threatened action, of the board of directors is beyond the authority conferred by the charter (as in the above example); or (2) that the transaction is so fraudulent as will result in serious injury to the corporation or to the interests of the other stockholders; or (3) that the board of directors, or a majority of them, are acting in their own interests, in a way destructive of the corporation itself, or of the other stockholders; or (4) that the majority of the stock-holders themselves are oppressively and illegally pursuing a course in violation of the rights of the other shareholders. Finally, it must appear that the aggrieved stockholder or stockholders have exhausted all means, within the corporation itself, to obtain redress of alleged grievances.

Question May stock be sold, mortgaged or pledged as security?

Answer Yes. One who buys stock usually stands in the same position as the one from whom he bought it.

Question How is stock transferred?

Answer Usually by indorsement and delivery of the stock certificate, its surrender at the office of the corporation, or to the transfer agent for a new certificate and the enrollment of the transferee (the person to whom the stock has been transferred) upon the books of the corporation as a stockholder.

Question Stockholders of a corporation agree among themselves not to sell, pledge or transfer their shares. Subsequently, the shareholder, in violation of this agreement, does sell his stock to a stranger. Is the transaction legal?

Answer Yes. An agreement between stockholders not to sell pledge or transfer their shares is in unreasonable restraint of trade and therefore void.

Question May a stockholder sell or transfer his shares to an infant -- that is, one under legal age?

Answer No, nor can he sell or transfer his stock to any person who is incapable in law of assuming liability with respect to shares, such as a lunatic, for example.

Question Does a transferee of stock have a right to vote at stockholders' meetings before he has had his transfer registered?

Answer   No. He also takes the risk, as against the corporation, of payment of the dividend to the person who appears as owner on the books of the corporation. Of course, the transferee would be entitled to recover dividends from the person so receiving them.

Question   What general powers do directors have?

Answer   Where general management of a corporation is entrusted to a board of directors or other officers, they have the power to bind the corporation by any act or contract within the powers conferred upon it. However, they cannot effect any great or radical change in organization without the assent of the stockholders, unless such power is expressly conferred. The board may delegate authority to a committee or to third persons to do acts for the company. They cannot delegate the exercise of a discretion vested in them.

Question   May a director vote upon any resolution in which he is personally interested?

Answer   No.

Question   May a director profit by his relationship to the corporation?

Answer   No. A director occupies a position of trust. He cannot use his position to make secret profits Without a full and fair disclosure of the facts.

Question   Jones, a tool manufacturer, sells some tools to a corporation of which he is a director, procuring the contract through his own vote. May the corporation cancel the contract?

Answer   Yes. If a director, by his own vote, procures a contract with himself in which his own interests are opposed to the corporation, the contract may be set aside by the corporation or its stockholders. The law does not permit a director to place himself in a position where he may betray the interests of the corporation to his own advantage.

Question   Are directors and other officers of a corporation personally liable for losses sustained by the corporation?

Answer   Ordinarily, directors are not personally liable for accidents, thefts, etc. where they have not been negligent, nor for mere mistakes or errors of judgment where they act in good faith and with ordinary care and diligence. However, they are personally liable if they willfully abuse their trust-as, by exceeding their authority or the powers of the corporation, or by misappropriating corporate funds. They are personally liable, too, when they are guilty of gross negligence and ma attention to the duties of their office.

Question How may a director be removed?

Answer By the stockholders of the corporation. He cannot be removed by his codirectors.

Question How may an officer of a corporation be removed?

Answer Normally, a corporation has a right to remove an officer or agent, where there is a contract for a fixed term, only where he violates his contract or is incompetent. But it can, at any time, revoke the authority of an agent, although it may render itself liable for breach of contract by so doing. An agent or officer who is appointed by vote of the stockholders, or whose term of office is fixed by charter, cannot be re moved, nor can his authority be revoked, by directors.

Question Jones, an investment broker, organizes and controls a number of corporations. He persuades his clients to invest in the worthless securities of these "dummy" corporations. A customer whom he has bilked now seeks to hold Jones personally liable. Jones defends on the ground that the corporation should be sued, not Jones. Is he right?

Answer No. There is a sharp difference between the legal rights and responsibilities of corporation and the legal rights and responsibilities of its members. Contracts made by an officer of a corporation, for example, bind the corporation, not the officer individually. Corporate debts are not the debts of its members but the debts of the corporation. However, when the corporate form is used as a cloak to evade responsibility, the court will ignore the corporate form and fix responsibility as substantial justice requires. Jones, therefore, would be liable individually.

Question A corporation issues a stock certificate to Jones, who claims that it is fully paid for. Jones sells it to a friend who has no idea that actually the stock is not fully paid for. Is the friend liable to creditors of the corporation?

Answer No, since the friend lacked knowledge.

Question Jones subscribes for stock of the par value of $1,000. He has paid but $200 on it when the corporation becomes in solvent. What can the creditors of the corporation collect from Jones?

Answer $800. The indebtedness of Jones is a corporate asset from which the corporation may meet its obligations.

Question   The president of a banking corporation enters into a coma tract with cotton brokers for the purchase of cotton on the stock exchange. The brokers buy the cotton for the bank president who, after due notice, refuses to receive the cotton. No money has passed between the parties. Is the bank liable?

Answer   No. The act of the president in contracting for the pure chase of cotton is beyond the usual scope of banking business; the bank, therefore, would not be liable. Had the cotton been delivered, however, the bank would be liable.

Question   Brown sues Smith for personal injuries resulting from a fall on a defective stairway in a corporation-owned building. Smith insists that the corporation be sued, not himself. Brown Contends, however, that the corporation holds title to the real estate merely as a subterfuge to relieve Smith, the real owner, from liability. The capital stock is $1,000, consisting of one hundred shares of a par value of $150 each, held by Smith and the members of his family. Who is liable, Smith or the corporation?

Answer   The corporation. Organizing a corporation for the purpose of escaping general liability is perfectly lawful. Hence, Smith is not liable, the corporation is.

Question   Four men contract to organize a corporation. It is agreed that Millman shall receive fifty shares of stock for installing a bookkeeping system for the proposed corporation. The next day, the corporation is organized, all its stock being issued to the four organizers. After this, Millman performs the services indicated but the corporation's officers refuse to deliver the promised shares of stock. Can they be compelled to do so?

Answer   Yes. A corporation is not usually liable for services and expenses of its promoters in organization. In the present-case, however, the evidence shows that the corporation adopted the contract, made by its organizers with Millman, and therefore is bound by it.

Question   A promoter promises to pay Jones for services rendered prior to incorporation. After the corporation is formed, Jones sues the corporation rather than the promoter, on the ground that the corporation benefitted by his services. May Jones recover from the corporation?

Answer	No. Prior to incorporation, a promoter is personally liable upon contracts made by him, unless he is acting as agent for the shareholders—in which case the shareholders would be liable: The promoter cannot represent the corporation or bind it, since the corporation is still non-existent. When the corporation comes into legal existence it may ratify the contract—in which case the corporation will be bound.
Question	A corporation contracts with a union to employ only union men and maintain a closed shop. In order to continue the same business with an open shop, the corporation discharges its men, discontinues its business and dissolves. The former shareholders then organize another corporation, carrying on business with the same shareholders, officers, etc., but employing non-union men. The union seeks to prevent the new corporation from violating the original agreement for a closed shop. May it do so?
Answer	Yes. Most states would regard the formation of the second corporation as a mere subterfuge to evade its contracted obligations.
Question	A railroad company buys a large office building which it then rents to tenants. Is this a proper exercise of its corporate powers?
Answer	Yes. Every corporation has a right to own as much property as is necessary to carry out its charter powers. In this case, it could be argued that the railroad company had an eye toward expansion. It could, therefore, erect a building to provide for such growth, although it was not then necessary.
Question	Does a corporation have the power to buy in its own shares?
Answer	Yes, when no harm is done to its creditors.
Question	May a corporation insure the lives of its officers?
Answer	Yes.
Question	Does a corporation have power to sell its assets?
Answer	Yes, if there is no dissent among the stockholders.
Question	May a stockholder object to a proposed merger or consolidation?
Answer	Courts generally refuse to allow a small minority to block a sale of assets, especially when the sale is to the interest of the stockholders. A dissenting stockholder, however, has a right to have his shares appraised in the manner provided by statute, and to receive payment therefor.

Question Under what circumstances may a receiver for a corporation be appointed?

Answer Usually, a receiver is appointed to take charge of the assets of a business where there is mismanagement or internal dissension in the corporation; where there is insolvency; or where the corporation is unable to pay its debts.

Question The president of a corporation signs a contract for advertising space in a magazine, for one year, at $1,000 per month. The president has not been authorized by his Board of Directors to sign the contract, nor is it signed by the general manager or secretary of the corporation. When the corporation refuses to pay the bill, it is sued by the magazine. Who will win?

Answer The corporation. Whether a president or any other corporate officer has authority to do particular acts depends upon the powers conferred upon him, either by the charter, the by-laws, or by the directors. In the absence of such authority, the president has no intrinsic power to bind the corporation.

Question Directors of a bank pass a resolution requiring that books should be opened, under-the direction of Atwell and Brown, for further subscription to the stock of the bank. It is agreed that $5 should be required on each share at the time of subscribing. Jones agrees to buy certain shares, arranging with Atwell and Brown that they take a note which Jones holds, then collect it, applying the proceeds to the payment of his, subscription. Learning of the transaction, the bank refuses to issue Atwell and Brown certificates of stock to the amount of Jones' subscription. Can the bank be legally compelled to do so?

Answer No. Atwell and Brown exceeded the authority conferred, upon them by the resolution. Having no authority to take anything but money for the stock, their act does not bind the bank, since it neither ratified nor affirmed the unauthorized transaction.

Question A farmer and his wife subscribe for stock, mortgaging their farm on representations that the stock will prove a lucrative investment. The stock goes down in value. The farmer and his wife now seek to repudiate the contract by returning the stock and obtaining the purchase price. Can they do so?

Answer   No. Opinions as to the value of stock are not such representations as are ordinarily a basis for repudiation of a contract.

Question   Directors of a corporation issue a prospectus stating that the company has a franchise to use steam power instead of horses on its right of way. Brown, relying on the representations, applies for and is allotted shares in the company. The corporation builds street railways, but, not obtaining the right to use steam power, it becomes insolvent. When Brown files suit against the corporation, it defends on the ground that the directors believed the truth of the assertion, although now they know it was false. Is this a good defense?

Answer   Yes. Unless it is proved that the false statements were made knowingly, or without belief in their truth, or with recite less disregard as to their truth or falsity, the corporation would not be bound. It is sufficient if the directors were motivated by the honest belief that their representations were true.

Question   Jones buys certain stock on a secret condition, agreed to by the promoter, that Jones will not be bound unless certain other parties subscribe. When the other parties fail to subscribe, Jones seeks to cancel his contract, alleging the secret condition which the promoter does not deny. May Jones cancel his agreement?

Answer   No. The capital stock of a corporation represents a fund paid in by its subscribers and stockholders so that it may conduct its business and pay its obligations. In the above example, Jones is imposing a condition which, if enforced, may deplete the fund to which creditors have a right to look for the payment of their debts. Hence, such secret conditions are void, and the subscription may be enforced against Jones.

Question   Do directors have power to dissolve a corporation?

Answer   No. It must be done by vote of the stockholders.

Question   How is a corporation dissolved?

Answer   1. If of limited duration, by the expiration of the term of its existence, fixed by charter or general law.

           2. By the loss of all its members, or of an integral part of the corporation, by death or otherwise, if the charter or act of incorporation provides no way by which such loss may

be supplied.

3. By the surrender of its corporate franchise to, and the acceptance by, the state authority.

4. By the forfeiture of its charter through the neglect of duties imposed or abuse of the privileges conferred by it, the forfeiture being enforced by proper legal action.

Advisory 10

TORTS

A tort is a private or civil wrong or injury.

In general, the law recognizes certain rights as belonging to every individual. There is the right to personal security, to liberty, to property, to reputation, to the services of a daughter or servant, to the companionship of a wife. Any violation of these rights is a tort. Similarly, the law recognizes certain duties as being obligatory with every individual was, for example, the duty of not deceiving another by false representation, of not persecuting another maliciously, of not using one's property to injure another. The violation of any of these duties, which results in damages, is also a tort.

The law of torts is concerned with the redress of injuries which are neither crimes nor arise from the breach of contracts. All acts or omissions of which the law takes notice are classed under the three heads of contracts, crimes and torts. The first includes agreements and the injuries resulting from their breach. Crimes include acts injurious to the public or state. Torts include injuries only to individuals. An act, however, may be both a tort and a crime at the same time., Assault and battery, a tort, may be likely to lead to a breach of the peace, thus becoming a matter of public concern and therefore a crime. Torts which are crimes at the same time include assault, libel and nuisance. In these cases, a public prosecution and a private action for damages may both be maintained, either at the same or at different times. The bulk of this chapter deals with negligence, one of the chief divisions of the law of torts. What is negligence? Negligence is the failure to exercise that degree of care which an ordinarily careful and prudent person exercises under the same or similar circumstances. Thus, the mere-fact that a person suffers a broken leg while alighting from a street car does not necessarily mean that he can collect from the transit company. To obtain a settlement or win a lawsuit, it must be shown that the operator of the street car was careless or reckless 1n its management. A case of negligence is made out, for example, when it is proved that the street car started off with a "sudden, violent and unusual jerk," or that the operator carelessly closed the door on the claimant's leg, or that there was some oily substance on the platform steps causing the claimant to fall. If, on the other hand, the accident was caused by the passenger's own clumsiness, a verdict will be returned in favor of the transit company. It follows, then, that before there can be a recovery in a personal injury case, two things must be proved: first, that the party making a claim or filing suit (the plaintiff) sustained some injury; second, that the party against whom a claim is being made (the defendant) was guilty of negligence in causing the accident. Whether a damage suit is won or lost often depends upon the quantity and quality of the witnesses. The more witnesses the plaintiff procures, the more he strengthens his case. A witness, to be effective, must not only be able to tell a credible story but must be able to bear up under the rigors of cross-examination. The best witnesses are those who give a simple, straightforward account of what happened, who are not easily shaken on cross-examination, and whose appearance and character are likely to impress a judge and jury. It is far better to have one good witness than five poor ones.

If you are unfortunate enough to get involved in accident, consult your attorney promptly. Don't try to handle the case yourself! Just as no sensible person would think of setting a broken leg without a physician, so no one ought to attempt to compromise a personal injury claim without profiting by the advice of an experienced lawyer.

One reason for this is that the average person has little idea of the value of his case. His demands are either excessive, in terms of the injuries received, or far below what they are usually worth. Trading on the credulity of claimants, some insurance adjusters are able to procure a settlement for a fraction of what the case should normally bring.

A striking example of this took place recently. Passing through a red traffic signal, one taxicab collided with another, injuring a passenger. As a result of the impact, Brown, the passenger, bruised his shoulder when thrown to the floor of the cab. Within the hour, an investigator called at the man's home and offered to settle with him for $50. After some bickering, the passenger signed a paper (release) relieving the taxicab company of all further liability, and accepted the $50.

Two weeks later, Brown noticed he was having trouble raising his arm. As the days passed, his shoulder became worse. Finally, alarmed, he consulted an orthopedic surgeon. X rays were taken and a diagnosis of arthritis was made. Apparently, Brown had had a dormant arthritis without suffering any degree of discomfort. According to the surgeon, the blow to the shoulder seriously aggravated the condition, eventually causing a fifty-per-cent permanent disability. And the case had been settled for $50!

Now for a few final cautions:
1. Consult a lawyer as soon as possible.

2. Don't sign any paper submitted by the defendant unless advised to do so by your attorney.

3. Make no verbal statement or admission to the defendant or his representative, relating either to the accident or your injuries, before seeing your lawyer.

4. Have photographs taken as soon as possible. Pictures showing the physical damage in an automobile collision and the point of impact between two vehicles are especially helpful. Have measurements made of skid marks, as skid marks are evidence of speed. Since a picture is more effective than any verbal statement, photographs of any defect alleged to be the cause of an accident should be taken promptly, particularly in cases involving a hole in the street or aide effective step in a house.

Question	Coming up close to Mary, John shakes a stick in her face, threatening to strike her, although he does not actually do so. Mary is frightened and, from the shock and fright, suffers a miscarriage. She files suit against John for damages. Does she have a claim?
Answer	Yes. John has committed an assault by threatening Mary with violence, accompanying his threats with menacing gestures. Such conduct is actionable, even though no physical injury results.
Question	Albert, without justification, bursts into Brenda's room in a hotel and uses violent and abusive language toward her. As a consequence of the nervous shock received through Albert's conduct, Brenda is made ill. Does she have a claim against Albert?
Answer	Yes. Mere insults and abuse do not amount to an assault if no violent touching is involved. In this case, however Brenda has suffered bodily harm.
Question	In the course of an argument you angrily point a loaded

pistol at Bill, threatening to shoot him. The gun is empty and you know it, but Bill does not. Bill sues you. May he recover?

Answer   Yes. Bill was put in fear of bodily harm, even though the gun was actually unloaded and the threat could not be carried out.

Question   As a joke, you tell Brenda that her husband has been killed in an automobile accident. The shock which this false statement gives Brenda, a rather nervous woman, brings on a serious illness. Are you liable in damages to Brenda?

Answer   Yes, since you should have foreseen that the intended fright might cause Brenda bodily injury. You would not be liable, however, if Brenda suffers fright without bodily injury.

Question   As a practical joke on Arthur, who is asleep on a beach, Jack holds a magnifying glass in such a way as to focus the sun's rays on Arthur's head. He keeps this up until Arthur awakes from the pain caused by the heat, and compels Jack to story. Arthur's head is severely burned. Does he have a claim against Jack?

Answer   Yes. Jack has committed a battery on Arthur by intentionally burning him. The fact that Jack did it as a joke does not excuse him.

Question   As a joke, Arthur throws a firecracker in front of an automobile which is being driven rapidly but within the speed limit. The explosion so startles the driver that he loses control of the car and swerves into a stone wall, injuring himself and the passengers. Is Arthur liable in damages?

Answer   Yes. Arthur knew, or should have known, that a sudden fright or shock is likely to cause the person subjected to it to react instinctively, without regard to the danger involved. In hurling the firecracker Arthur was the proximate cause of the injuries.

Question   Arthur has a legal right to enter a certain building. To keep Arthur out, Bill locks all the doors and windows so that Arthur is unable to get in. Arthur sues Bill for false imprisonment. Can he recover?

Answer   No. To constitute an imprisonment it is necessary that a person be confined. In this case, Arthur is not confined, since he is at liberty to go anywhere in the world—except the particular place from which he is barred.

Question	James is asleep in a room high above the ground, with no available means of exit but one door. Bill, knowing James is in the room, locks the door from the outside, though he has no legal authority to do so. Before James awakes, Bill unlocks the door so that when James is ready to leave, he is able to do so. Later, James, learning that Bill locked him in the room, files suit against him. Can he recover?
Answer	No. If James had tried to get out and had been unable to do so because he was locked in, he would have had a claim against Bill, but since James was unaware of any restraint, he could suffer no injury for which he could be compensated.
Question	Arthur locks the door of the room in which Bill is sitting. Arthur knows, but believes Bill does not know, that there is an unlocked but concealed door through which Bill could, if he knew it, escape. Bill does not know of the unlocked door. Does Bill have a claim against Arthur?
Answer	Yes. Bill has been unlawfully deprived of his liberty.
Question	Arthur is a patron in Jack's restaurant. As Arthur is about to leave, Jack tells him to wait while an investigation, is made to determine whether or not Arthur paid his bill. When it is learned that Arthur did actually pay, he is allowed to go. Does Arthur have a claim against Jack for false imprisonment?
Answer	Yes, if the jury finds that Arthur was detained for an unreasonable time or in an unreasonable way. Otherwise, no.
Question	You buy a bottle of peroxide which, when you uncork it, explodes and causes you personal injuries. Against whom do you have a claim?
Answer	You may sue the manufacturer. You may also have a claim against the retailer if you can prove that he was negligent in selling the peroxide to you.
Question	You buy a heating pad which, through faulty construction, gives off an excessive amount of heat, causing a severe burn. Against whom do you have a claim?
Answer	Both the manufacturer and the seller of the heating pad are liable.
Question	At a seaside resort, a beach umbrella, blown through the air, strikes and injures Bill. Is the resort liable?
Answer	Yes. The danger of such a happening should reasonably have been foreseen by the management.
Question	Your wife goes to a beauty shop to get a permanent wave.

	In the course of the treatment she suffers scalp burns. Is the beauty shop owner liable in damages?
Answer	Yes. A beauty shop proprietor is under a duty to exercise the care which a reasonably prudent and skillful person gaged in the same calling would exercise under the same of similar circumstances.
Question	You buy a soft drink from a confectionery store. While drinking its contents, you discover that a small mouse had somehow gotten into the bottle. You become ill and seek to recover damages against the manufacturer. Can you?
Answer	Yes. A manufacturer of beverages is liable to the consumer for any injuries resulting from impurities in the beverage. However, if the manufacturer can prove, as he usually does, that he used the care, skill and diligence in and about the manufacturing and bottling of the soft drink that a reasonably careful, skillful and diligent person engaged in a similar business would use, that is all the law requires and the plaintiff is barred from recovery.
Question	Smith manufactures and places on the market a patent medicine. The dose prescribed on the bottle contains mercury in poisonous quantities. You purchase a bottle of the medicine and your wife, taking the prescribed dose, is made seriously ill. Is the manufacturer liable to your wife?
Answer	Yes. The negligence of the manufacturer consists in the fact that the dosage labelled on the bottle is misleading.
Question	You are a customer in a department store. You walk through the aisle, looking at goods displayed on the counters. While doing so, you stumble over an obstruction in the aisle— which you could have seen had you been looking at the floor instead of at the goods on the counter. Is the department store liable?
Answer	Yes. You are entitled to rely on the fact that the aisle is reasonably safe for patrons of the store.
Question	While walking down the stairway of a department store, you slip, falling on your back. May the department store be held liable?
Answer	No. The department store or its servants must have been negligent in some way before liability can be established. If, for example, your falling is caused by the existence of an oily substance which the employees. of the store negligently fail to remove, the store would be liable.
Question	While walking down the aisle of a motion picture theater,

you stumble and fall over a piece of torn carpet, injuring yourself. Is the theater liable?

Answer   Yes; if you can show that the condition of the carpet was known to the owner of the theater, or had existed for such a length of time that the theater owner should have known of it.

Question   A boy gains admission to a circus by crawling under the canvas. While seated with the paying patrons, he is injured by the negligence of one of the clowns who explodes a giant cracker too near the audience. Is the circus liable for the boy's injuries?

Answer   Yes. The circus has a duty to exercise reasonable care in conducting its activities so as to avoid causing bodily harm to those even wrongfully on the premises.

Question   John, who operates a hotel, employs Bill as a plumber to install a shower bath. Bill negligently transposes. the handles so that the hot water pipe is labeled "cold." A guest, deceived by the label, turns on the hot water and is scalded. Is the hotel liable?

Answer   Yes. John is as liable as if he had done the work himself instead of entrusting it to the plumber.

Question   Arthur tells his dentist to extract a particular tooth. Having given Arthur an anesthetic, the dentist discovers a cavity in an adjoining tooth which he rightly concludes to be the case of the ache. He pulls the adjoining tooth. Does Arthur have a cause of action against the dentist?

Answer   Yes. Arthur directed the dentist to extract one particular tooth. The fact that he would have consented to the extraction of a different tooth is immaterial. If the arrangement had been for the dentist to extract a tooth which, in his opinion, was the cause of Arthur's pain, Arthur would have no claim, since he gave his consent to the dentist's action. In the absence of such an arrangement, the dentist is liable. The same principle of law is true in surgical operations. An operation performed on a patient without his consent is action able at law, since it is an invasion of the rights of another.

Question   Arthur suffers from a disease of his right kidney. His physician advises him to submit to an operation for its removal, but Arthur refuses. Later, Arthur consents to another minor operation and, for that purpose, submits to anesthesia. The physician removes Arthur's kidney. Does

	Arthur have a claim against the physician?
Answer	Yes. An unlawful "battery" against Arthur's body has taken place.
Question	Arthur goes to a hospital for an appendectomy and is taken to the operating room. By a mistake of the hospital force, the surgeon who is to operate on Arthur is given the record of Charles, instead. Charles' record calls for an operation upon a tumor on his back. Misled by this error, the surgeon makes an incision in Arthur's back before the error is discovered. Is the surgeon liable?
Answer	Yes. The unauthorized operation is an invasion of the patient's privacy for which the surgeon is held accountable.
Question	Your dentist fails to remove part of the root of a tooth extracted by him. He tells you, however, that he has done so. As a result, your jaw becomes infected and you are hospitalized for a few weeks. Can the dentist be charged with negligence?
Answer	Yes. Dentists have been held liable for improper treatment of a cavity after extraction, resulting in infection; use of unsterilized instruments; improper removal of an impacted tooth; unnecessarily removing several healthy teeth and failure to stem the flow of blood from an artery following an extraction. A dentist, like a physician, is not liable, however, for errors of judgment where the proper course is reasonably doubtful.
Question	Arthur and Bill are players on opposite sides in a football game. In the course of the game, Bill tackles Arthur who is injured. Does Arthur have a claim?
Answer	No. By participating in the game Arthur assumes the risks that go with it and to which the law implies that he gave his consent.
Question	Arthur, age eight, in company with a group of other boys, repeatedly plays on Bill's lumber pile kept on Bill's land. Bill has often ordered the boys off the premises, Arthur himself having been ejected several times. Seeing the boys on the pile of lumber, Bill picks up a stick and runs toward them, shaking the stick and shouting to them to "Get out of there." Arthur, frightened, runs out into the near-by street. There he is struck by a passing automobile which is being operated with reasonable care. Is Bill liable in damages?
Answer	No. The boy is a trespasser and Bill may employ reasonable

force, if necessary, to expel a trespasser from the premises, though he cannot kill him or indict serious bodily harm.

Question Arthur, holding a cane, is standing on the road. Bill, a one-legged man, flourishes a knife and threatens to attack Arthur. Arthur stands his ground. When Bill comes close, he strikes Bill's leg with his cane, so that he falls on the ground and is bruised. Arthur could have avoided the whole incident by going into his house a short distance away and locking the door. Is he liable to Bill for damages?

Answer No. One may use such force in self-defense as appears reasonably necessary under the circumstances.

Question Arthur attacks Bill upon the street. Bill raises his cane to ward off Arthur's attack and, in so doing, strikes Charles, a bystander. Is Arthur or Bill liable in damages?

Answer Arthur, because he is the proximate cause of Charles' injuries.

Question Arthur, a small boy, throws a snowball at Bill. He hits Bill in the eye, causing him severe pain. May Bill, in retaliation, "beat up" Arthur?

Answer No, not unless he believes that Arthur will continue to throw snowballs at him. Should Arthur do so, Bill has a right to use force to compel the boy to desist, an assault and battery having been committed.

Question John is a guest at the Hillside Hotel. At John's invitation, Bill goes to the hotel, visits John in his room and plays cards for money. Gambling is a criminal offense in this particular
state. The elevator shaft in the hotel is in a dark place and, on leaving, Bill sustains injuries by falling into the open elevator shaft when he thinks he is stepping into the elevator itself. Does Bill have a claim against the hotel?

Answer No. To a guest in a hotel the innkeeper has an obligation to use due care to keep the premises reasonably safe and to discover and remove dangerous conditions. He owes the same duty to one who comes on proper business with a hotel guest—as, for example, to a merchant who comes to inspect a salesman's samples or to a friend who comes to pay a social call. In this case, however, Bill has come for an unlawful purpose, not on proper business of the hotel or the guest; therefore, he cannot claim the benefit of the duty owed an invited guest whose business is lawful. Bill is a mere trespasser to whom the hotel owes no duty save to actively refrain from injuring him.

Question	You invite Bill to your house for dinner. As Bill starts to ring your doorbell, his leg goes through the porch floor, due to the defective condition of the porch. The defect is unknown to you. Are you liable to Bill?

Answer	No. Bill can recover only for such defects as are known to the occupant of the house. You owe no duty to inspect for concealed dangers. If Bill does sue you, you can defend on the ground that you did not know the porch floor was defective. If evidence is produced to the contrary, the question becomes one of fact to be resolved by a jury or by the court sitting as a jury. The burden of proof is on Bill to show that you had knowledge of the defect. If he can offer no such evidence, he will lose his case.

Question	You lend Bill your automobile to go for a ride. The car is defective and, while Bill is driving it, he is injured. You do not know of the defect. Does Bill have a claim against you?

Answer	No. If you had loaned the car with a hidden defect to Bill, for a consideration, you would have been liable. But one who lends a car without receiving anything of value in return (the consideration) is not liable, except for defects which he knows and should recognize as making the car dangerous to use.

Question	The Dixie Motor Car Company sells automobiles which are assembled from parts purchased from other manufacturers. The Dixie Company buys the chassis, including brake mechanics, from the Boston Company. Through the Boston Company's negligence, the brakes in one car are defective. The Dixie Company could have discovered the defect if a reasonable inspection had been made, but it was not. Once the car is assembled, the defect is not discoverable unless the entire car is torn down. The Dixie Company sells the car to the Charles Company, dealer in automobiles. The Charles Company then sells the car to Paul, a retail customer. When Paul is driving the car carefully, he collides with Smith's automobile, which is also being driven carefully, because of the defective brakes. Smith is hurt. Against whom does Smith have a claim?

Answer	The Boston Company. Paul is not liable because he was driving carefully. The Boston Company is responsible for the accident, since it allowed the car to go out with defective brakes, the proximate cause of the collision.

Question A boiler insurance company, as part of its service, under takes to inspect your boiler. It issues a certificate that the boiler is fit for use. Relying upon this certificate, you use the boiler. It explodes, due to a defect which a reasonably careful inspection would have disclosed. The explosion wrecks the adjacent building, causing the occupants therein bodily harm. Who is liable?

Answer The boiler insurance company. If it is part of a person's business or profession to give information or advice regarding matters upon which the personal safety of another depends, he must exercise reasonable care that the information is sufficiently accurate to insure the safety of such persons. The boiler company was negligent in failing to find a defect which could have been discovered.

Question Arthur's house contains a mass of oil-soaked rags in a corner of his basement. The rags take fire spontaneously, the tire spreading to Burt's house next door. Is Arthur liable to Burt whose house has been partially destroyed by fire?

Answer Yes. Arthur would be charged with knowledge of the combustible quality of the rags, although he may be actually ignorant of that fact.

Question You own a flock of chickens. Your neighbor, who lives across the road from you, has a freshly-planted garden. Although your yard is enclosed by a fence, your chickens get out, go into your neighbor's garden and cause considerable damage before they can be removed. Your neighbor now seeks to hold you liable. Can he?

Answer Yes. The rule is that an owner of animals is liable for trespass committed by them, even though he uses due care to keep them restrained.

Question Richard, a broker, buys a farm through his agent; the agent telling him that the farm is a sound investment. Later, needing money, Richard decides to sell the farm. He has never seen the property, Richard. tells Harry, an inexperienced young man who has just inherited some money, that the farm contains good corn land, is a sound investment and will provide Harry with an income. Harry, without further investigation, relying on Richard's recommendation, buys the farm for $15,000. It is not good corn land and is worth only $50,000. Harry now seeks to recover his money. May he?

Answer   Yes. Richard misrepresented the facts. He had never seen the farm and therefore knew nothing of it; yet he stated specifically that it was good corn land.

Question   A state law declares that any man having sexual intercourse with a girl under eighteen years of age, not his wife, is guilty of rape, regardless of whether or not the girl consents. The law is silent on the subject of civil liability. Arthur has intercourse with Bernice, who is under eighteen, but with her consent. Does Bernice have a claim for damages against Arthur?

Answer   Yes. Such a law is designed to protect young girls from the consequences of their own act.

Question   A strong swimmer sees a man floundering in deep water. Not knowing the man's identity, he goes to his rescue. When he discovers that the drowning man is a man whom he hates, the swimmer turns away, letting the other man drown. Is the swimmer liable in damages?

Answer   No. A person is under no legal duty to aid or protect another who has fallen into peril through no fault of the former.

Question   You see a blind man about to step into the street in front of an approaching automobile. You could prevent him from doing so, by a word or touch, without delaying your own progress. Yet you do not do so. The blind man is run over and hurt. Can you be held liable?

Answer   No. There is no legal duty imposed on you to go to the blind man's rescue.

Question   John operates a private sanitarium for the insane. Through the negligence of the guards employed by him, a homicidal maniac escapes and attacks Bill, a stranger. Is the hospital liable?

Answer   Yes. One who voluntarily takes charge of a person who he knows, or should know, is likely to cause bodily harm to others if not controlled is liable in damages to the person harmed.

Question   John, a guest in your house, is seriously ill and in need of immediate medical attention. You call your physician on the telephone, the physician promising to come immediately, thereby causing you not to summon other medical aid. The physician neglects to come until several hours later. As a result, John's illness is aggravated, due to lack of immediate attention. Is the physician liable?

Answer   Yes. He is liable in damages for the aggravation of the illness. John had a right to rely on the promise that the physician would come promptly. The latter was negligent in failing to come as promised, or, at the very least, notifying John that he would be tardy so that another physician might be called.

Question A mining company knows that children in the neighborhood are in the habit of playing around the mouth of a pit. One of the employees of the company leaves a cartridge of blasting powder lying in a shed which the children, to the knowledge of the company, have used as a playhouse. Youngsters, coming to play, find the cartridge and use it as a plaything. They cause it to explode, the explosion injuring one of the children. Is the mining company liable?

Answer   Yes. The company officials knew that the children were likely to trespass around the mouth of the pit. To knowingly leave dynamite under such circumstances is negligence.

Question A manufacturing. company permits the children of its workmen to enter the factory in order to bring their fathers' lunch to them. A daughter of one of the employees comes into the factory for this purpose. While there she is hurt, due to the careless manner in which some of the workmen of the company do their work. Is the company liable for injuries sustained by the daughter?

Answer   Yes. In the above case, the daughter is legally called a "licensee," this being a person privileged to enter or remain upon land with the landlord's consent, whether given by invitation or permission. To such persons the company would be liable for bodily harm caused by failure to carry on activities with reasonable care.

Question During rush hours, the passengers on a street car are accustomed to crowd into it in a way likely to cause injury. The company fails to provide a sufficient staff of guards to me vent this practice. A passenger, hurt during a rush hour, files a claim against the street railway company. Is the company liable?

Answer   Yes. Having knowledge of the crowded condition, it becomes necessary for the company to take active steps to prevent it. If a passenger is hurt as a result of its failure to provide the necessary guards, the company will be liable.

Question John employs a building contractor to build a row of houses according to certain plans and specifications supplied by John. These plans require material and workmanship so cheap and inferior that any competent builder would realize that houses so built might collapse at any time. The com tractor builds the houses under these plans and specifications. One of the homes collapses, thereby causing injury to a prospective purchaser. Is the contractor liable?

Answer   Yes. Liability is based on the fact that the contractor knew that the house would not be reasonably safe. When, nevertheless, he went ahead and erected it, he made himself liable to those lawfully on the premises who might be injured.

Question   While moving his household goods, Arthur throws out of his window a heavy parcel, intending it to fall into a waiting cart. Before doing so, he calls out, "Watch out below." His aim misses, however, and the parcel falls onto the sidewalk, striking a pedestrian who did not hear the warning because his attention was directed to other matters. Is Arthur liable to the pedestrian?

Answer   Yes. The fact that Arthur shouted a warning does not relieve him from liability. In throwing the parcel out of the window, he is acting in a reckless manner and must assume the responsibility for the consequences of his act. Arthur should have waited until the sidewalk was actually clear of pedestrians before throwing out the parcel.

Question   A blind man walks along a sidewalk in which there is a hole. A normal man would see the hole and avoid it, but the blind man stumbles and falls as a consequence of walking into it. Does he have a claim against the city for his injuries, assuming that the city paved the walk?

Answer   Yes. The law makes allowance for physical defects which prevent a person from seeing, or acting in the way a normal person would.

Question   While crossing a street at night, you step into a hole, falling and breaking your arm. Do you have a claim against the city?

Answer   Yes, if you can show that the hole or defect was in the street for a sufficiently long time to have provided the city with notice of the defect, thus affording it an opportunity to repair it.

Question   Suppose the accident had occurred in the daytime. Would you still have a claim?

Answer   Yes, but not a strong one. The principle is that, in the daytime, you could have avoided the hole if you had looked. Failing to look might make you guilty of contributing to the accident.

Question Bill boards a crowded street car, dropping his fare in the box. The conductor fails to notice that Bill has paid his fare and demands that he deposit another coin. Upon Bill's refusal, the conductor bodily removes him. Does Bill have a claim against the transit company?

Answer No. If a passenger refuses to pay his lawful fare or to give proper evidence that he has paid it, he may be ejected from the car. However, if Bill, through witnesses, could prove that he did in fact pay his fare and was therefore wrongfully removed from the car, he would have a valid claim against the transit company.

Question A young girl is a train passenger, holding a ticket to Baltimore. Falling asleep, she is carried beyond her station. The conductor asks for additional fare, but the girl, having no money, is unable to pay it. The conductor at once stops the train and puts the girl off. The place at which she is put off is an isolated spot near the camp of a construction gang. It is a notorious fact that many of this gang are of a rough and violent character. The girl is ravished by a member of this gang. Is the railroad liable?

Answer Yes. The railroad is guilty of negligence in ejecting the girl at a place which it knew, or should have known, was dangerous, thus affording an opportunity for misconduct.

Question A telegraph company receives a message sent by Thompson, a wholesaler, calling for the delivery of five hundred bicycles. The message, reading, "five bicycles," is delivered to the bicycle manufacturer who fills the order for five bicycles. As a result of the altered telegram, Thompson is unable to fill his five hundred orders. Does he have a claim against the telegraph company?

Answer Yes. A message must be delivered exactly as furnished. For any alteration for which damages are sustained, a telegraph company is liable.

Question Who has the right of way at an intersection, a motorist or pedestrian?

Answer Pedestrian.

Question Who has the right of way between intersections, a motorist or pedestrian?

Answer Motorist.

Question While crossing a street, not at the intersection, a pedestrian is struck by a motorist. Is the pedestrian barred from recovering?

Answer Theoretically, no. A pedestrian may cross a street wherever he chooses, but the fact that he does not cross at the proper place is something the jury will take into consideration in arriving at a verdict. In the above example, the likelihood of the pedestrian collecting damages is much less than if he had been struck while crossing the intersection.

Question Who has the right of way at an intersection controlled by traffic signals?

Answer The one having the green light. Where the traffic signals are not in operation at an intersection the pedestrian has the right of way over the motorist.

Question Arthur, who has just obtained his driver's license, takes Bill for a ride in the country. While driving along a narrow stretch of road, Arthur's car runs off the paving onto the dirt shoulder. In maneuvering to regain the roadway, the car is overturned, due to Arthur's inexperience as a driver. Does Bill have a cause of action?

Answer No. Arthur is only required to use a degree of care which would be reasonable to expect from a beginner and not from the ordinary driver. Having done his best, Arthur is not liable.

Question Dan invites Paul, as his guest, to take a drive in his automobile. Paul accepts the invitation. Due to Dan's negligence in handling the car, it collides with a truck and Paul is hurt. Paul now seeks to hold Dan liable. May he?

Answer Yes, in the absence of a state law to the contrary. Dan owes Paul reasonable care in driving the automobile, even though Paul is a guest and not a paid passenger. In at least half the states, however, by statute a guest may recover only where the driver has been guilty of "gross negligence," "recklessness" or "willful or wanton misconduct."

Question In the above case, suppose that Paul has been hurt by the combined negligence of Dan and the truck driver. Could Paul recover against both?

Answer Yes.

Question Arthur invites Bill, as his guest, to take a drive-in Arthur's automobile. Bill accepts. Due to Arthur's negligence in handling the car, it collides with a truck and Bill is hurt.

Arthur has been driving at an excessive rate of speed. Bill knew it and said or did nothing. The excessive speed is a proximate cause of the collision in which Bill is hurt. Can Bill recover from Arthur?

Answer   Probably not. A guest must use due care for his own safety if he is to recover against another for injuries sustained by the other's negligence. Thus, if one rides with a driver known to be intoxicated, he is careless and cannot recover. Bill should have cautioned Arthur to cut down on his speed.

Question Paul, owner of an automobile, parks it and leaves Dan, his friend in the car in an intoxicated condition, with the ignition key in place. During Paul's absence, Dan attempts to drive the car away without the consent of Paul and negligently wrecks it. Paul now sues Dan. May he recover?

Answer   Yes. Dan's act is an intentional wrong and Paul may recover from Dan.

Question Paul, a youngster of three years, is left unattended on a busy street by his parents. He suffers injuries when struck by an automobile. Do Paul's parents have a claim against the driver, assuming the latter is negligent?

Answer   Yes. Paul is too young to be held responsible for his parents' carelessness in leaving him unattended.

Question Albert violates a traffic ordinance by parking his car on the wrong side of a street. Bertram, a five-year-old child, runs out from behind Albert's car and is killed by a passing automobile—through no fault of the driver. The evidence shows that if Albert's car had been legally parked, facing in the opposite direction, the obstacle to the child's vision and that of the driver of the passing car would have been as great as it was with Albert's car illegally parked. Do the parents of Bertram have a claim against Albert?

Answer   No. Since Albert's car would have been an equally great obstacle to the vision of both the child and the passing driver, whether facing in the proper direction or not, it is clear that Albert's act of parking his car the wrong way did not cause the accident.

Question Arthur is seated on his doorstep, in front of which children are playing, ball on the sidewalk. Burt is driving his car down the street at a legal rate of speed. He sees the children but does not slacken speed or bring the car under more perfect control. One of the children darts into the street in pursuit of the ball. Arthur, seeing this and realizing that

Burt will be unable to stop the car in time to avoid running down the child, dashes forward, pulling the child out of danger. However, he slips and falls under the car which runs over him, breaking his leg. Is the driver liable to Arthur?

Answer   Yes. Burt is under a legal obligation both to slacken his speed and to obtain a better degree of control of his car when he sees the children. In this he is negligent. Arthur's injuries are caused by his attempt to prevent the child from being so run down; therefore, Burt would be liable in damages to Arthur.

Question   You permit a sixteen-year-old girl to drive your car, knowing that she has never driven before. She drives the car with you in it. While doing so, she causes a collision with John's car. As a result, John is hurt. John files suit against you. Can he recover?

Answer   Yes. It is negligence to permit one to use a thing or to engage in an activity under your control if you know, or should know, that such person is likely to use the thing, or to conduct himself in such a manner as to create an unreasonable risk of harm to others.

Question   You permit your chauffeur, who is in the habit of driving at an excessive rate of speed, to use your car to take his family to the seashore. While driving the car for this purpose, the chauffeur drives recklessly, injuring Paul, a pedestrian. Against whom has Paul a claim?

Answer   Against both you and the chauffeur. You are negligent in permitting him to have the car when you know his habit of excessive speed. For whatever it is worth, the chauffeur may also be held.

Question   You hire a taxicab and, telling the driver that you have but ten minutes to catch your train, you direct him to ignore traffic signals. You offer him $10 if he will get you to the station in time for the train. While the driver is speeding, the taxicab collides with Bill's car, causing personal injuries to him. Are you liable?

Answer   Yes. You knew, or should have known, that obedience to your orders was likely to cause harm.

Question   Bill negligently runs you down in his automobile, breaking your leg. A few weeks after the accident, Bill becomes insane. May he still be sued for damages?

Answer   Yes. Insanity would be no defense, even if it were proved that Bill was insane at the time of the accident.

Question   While carefully driving your automobile along a public highway, you accidentally go over a fairly large hole, causing a tire to blow out. Because you. are unable to properly control the car, it goes into a ditch. As a result, your wife strikes her head against the windshield, Does your wife have a claim against the city?

Answer   Yes. You may also recover damage for your tire.

Question   Albert is driving his automobile on a public highway. He is operating his car without a license and without having license plates attached to the car, but he is driving it with due care. While so driving, the car falls through an unsafe bridge and Albert is hurt. The condition of the bridge is due to the city's negligence, the city officials having had sufficient notice of the defect. Is the city liable?

Answer   Yes. It is true that Albert violated the law by not having secured the required license, but the car would have fallen through the bridge just as readily, whether it bore license plates or not.

Question   Driving his automobile at five miles per hour across a railroad track, Albert stalls on the crossing. The engineer on the approaching train carelessly fails to keep a lookout and a collision results. If he had done so, he would have discovered Albert's plight in time to avoid the accident. Can Albert recover, in spite of his contributory negligence?

Answer   Probably. The engineer, by using due care, might have avoided the accident, even though Albert contributed towards its happening. Having had the "last clear chance" to avoid the accident and failing to avail himself of it, the engineer is guilty of negligence and the railroad company would be liable.

Question   An engineer of a locomotive is driving it with the throttle open. on rounding a curve, he sees a trespasser lying on the track a quarter of a mile away. The train runs over the man, killing him. Is the railroad liable?

Answer   Yes. The engineer, by slackening the speed, could have stepped the train in time without injury to its passengers. In failing to do so, the engineer is guilty of negligence.

Question   Through the negligence of a railroad company, Bill sustains a compound fracture of his leg. Despite proper medical attention, Bill never regains the full use of his leg. After his doctors have advised him that he can again walk, the bad condition of his leg causes him to fall and break his arm while crossing a pavement which, had his leg been normal, he would have traversed safely. Bill now seeks to recover damages against the railroad both for the injury to his leg and for his broken arm. Can he?

Answer   Yes. If a company is liable for an injury which impairs the physical condition of a person's body, it is also liable for harm sustained in a later accident which would not have occurred had the person's bodily efficiency not been impaired.

Question   Bill attempts to drive his automobile across a track, in full view of an approaching locomotive, in the belief that he has ample time to cross. Misjudging the train's speed, Bill's car is struck by the locomotive and Bill sustains serious personal injuries. He now seeks to collect damages from the railroad. Can he?

Answer   No. By driving across the track in full view of map preaching locomotive, Bill is guilty of contributory negligence. His duty is to "stop, look and listen" before proceeding. By failing to do so he assumes the risk involved.

Question   Albert is a passenger in a motor bus operated by Ben. At an intersection Ben negligently drives the bus on the railroad tracks in front of an approaching train. The gates at the intersection are lowered as Ben goes on the track, making it impossible for him to proceed in either direction. The train crew sees the bus and its peril, but negligently fails to take precautions to stop the train quickly enough to prevent a collision. The train could have been stopped had its crew used care as soon as the danger was discovered. Albert, the passenger of the bus, is hurt in the resulting collision. From whom may he recover, if anyone?

Answer   He may recover from both Ben and the railroad. Ben is negligent in running the bus upon the tracks in front of the train. The train is negligent in running into the bus. The combined negligence of both caused Albert's injuries.

Question   In the above example, suppose the bus itself is injured in the collision. Can Ben, the driver, recover against the railroad?

Answer   Yes. While he is negligent, his negligence leaves him in a position where he is powerless to avoid the accident. By the exercise of due care at the critical moment, the train could have avoided the catastrophe.

Question   A motorman of a street car sees a man walking down the tracks. Although he has time to stop the car, he realizes that if he does, the sudden stopping might injure the passengers on the crowded street car. When-the man is first seen by the motorman there is a reasonable chance that he will himself observe the oncoming car in time to reach a place of safety. The motorman does not put on the emergency brakes. The man does not leave the tracks and is run down by the street car. Is the street car company liable?

Answer   No. Here, the motorman is faced with the alternative of either running down the man, to whom he owes no duty at all except to refrain from actively harming him, or of possibly derailing the street car by a sudden stoppage, thus causing injury to its passengers to whom it owes the highest degree of care.

Question   After you board a street car, the car starts off with a sudden and violent jerk which throws you to the floor, injuring your back. Is the transit company liable?

Answer   Yes. All carriers of passengers (buses, boats, trains, etc.) While not insurers of their passengers' safety, owe them the highest practical degree of care. Where a fall or other injury is caused by a sudden, severe and unusual jerk, the carrier is liable.

Question   Within what time from the date of the accident can you file suit?

Answer   Generally, within three years.

Advisory 11

WILLS

A WILL, directing as it does the disposition of your proper after death, is one of the most important documents you will ever be called upon to write. Therefore, in writing you will the following precautions should be observed, lest it will become involved in costly litigation or even, perhaps be Completely upset after your death. (1) Never write a Will while under the influence of liquor. If it can later be proven that you did so, the chances are excellent that your will will not be worth the paper it is written on. (2) Avoid eccentric bequests as much as possible. Leaving a large sum of money to a favorite pet may be seized upon as evidence of a lack of mental capacity. If you insist on making a bequest which may later appear to be odd, state your reason clearly for doing so, since the more rational your reasons the less likelihood is there that your will may be upset. (3) Choose carefully the person who is to write your will. A will is a complex legal document and should be entrusted only to the hands of a lawyer. If you must write your own will, have it checked carefully by an experienced attorney to see that it legally expresses your wishes. (4) Make certain that the property you leave is accurately described and located; also include the interest in the property the recipients are to receive, together with their full names and addresses; if you do not, there is a chance that they may not receive it at all. (5) Name as executor someone in whom you have the utmost confidence. A good practice is to nominate two executors—for example, your attorney and your closest relative in whom you have implicit trust. (6) Comply with the law of your particular state as to the presence of witnesses, method of attestation (witnessing), number of witnesses and their competency; select carefully those who are to witness your will, remembering that they may have to testify in court after your death. (7) After your will has been duly executed, do not allow any alteration unless absolutely necessary. Changes wrongfully made may upset the entire document. (8) Remember that marriage and the birth of a child revokes a will already made. (9) In revoking a will the safest method is to burn and completely destroy the document unless you intend it to take effect after your death, never leave an old will lying around where it may be discovered after your demise. (10) Don't try to cut off your spouse completely in your will. It can't be done, since she (or he) is entitled to a share of your estate, under statute law. Most states also provide that the surviving spouse may elect to take, either under the will or as the local statute permits. If, under a statute, your wife is entitled to a third of your estate, she will still receive her share, even though you leave her nothing in your will. (11) Last, but by no means least, keep your will in a safe place. A sound practice is to entrust the document to the probate court for safekeeping.

Question   What is a will?

Answer   A will is an instrument by which a person makes a disposition of his property to take effect after his death.

Question   What happens to your property if you die in the state—that is, without a will?

Answer   Instead of being disposed of according to your wishes, your property is distributed in accordance with the law of your particular state which may be contrary to your express wishes. When you leave a will, your estate is managed. by the executor named by you. When you die without a will, the court will appoint an administrator, usually your closest relative, who might not be your personal choice had you given the matter some thought.

Question   What is a testator?

Answer   A testator is a man who has made a will.

Question   What is a testatrix?

Answer   A testatrix is a woman who has made a will.

Question   What is meant by a codicil to a will?

Answer   A codicil is a supplement or addition to a will, made by the testator or testatrix, by which the dispositions in the will are explained, added to or altered.

Question   What is a devise?

Answer   A devise is real property passing under a will—for example, a house.

Question   What is a devisee?

Answer   A devisee is the person who takes real property under a will.

Question   What is a legacy?

Answer   A legacy is personal property passing under a will, especially money.

Question   What is a bequest?

Answer   A bequest is any form of personal property passing under a will-as, for example, a collection of books, a piano, etc.

Question   What is a legatee?

Answer   The person who takes personal property under a will.

Question   What is a beneficiary under a will?

Answer   A person who receives a benefit or advantage under a will.

Question   What is the difference between an executor and administrator of a will?

Answer   An executor is one named in the will by the testator to carry out its provisions. An administrator, on the other hand, is one appointed by the court to administer the estate of the deceased where there is no will.

Question   In making a will, whom should you generally appoint as executor?

Answer   Your attorney, if you have one, or your wife, husband or child to act as co-executor with your lawyer. It is a good idea to include in your will an alternate executor, to be appointed upon the death of the executor named by you.

Question   May an executor refuse to accept appointment under a will?

Answer   Yes.

Question   What happens when the executor named in the will dies before the testator?

Answer   A new executor should be named by the testator. Should the executor die after the testator, a new executor will be appointed by the court where the will does not provide an alternate.

Question   Who is usually appointed administrator?

Answer   Ordinarily, preference is given in the following order: the widow or widower; son or daughter; grandchild, father or mother, brother or sister; and finally, any other next of kin, preferably the one taking the largest share of the estate.

Question   How is an executor named in the will, or an administrator appointed by the court, paid?

Answer   The executor or administrator is paid a commission which is deducted from the estate. Though statutes vary in different states, the usual commission is up to ten per cent of the value of the estate.

Question   May an executor or administrator be removed from office?

Answer   Yes, if he reveals himself to be corrupt or manifestly incompetent.

Question   At what age is a person legally competent to make a will?

Answer   In Alabama the age is twenty-one years for disposing of real estate and eighteen years for disposing of personal property. The age is twenty-one in Alaska and Arizona for both real estate and personal property. In Arkansas anyone over twenty-one may leave real estate and personal property. by will; anyone over eighteen may bequeath personal property. California requires a person to be eighteen years or over to dispose of real estate and personal property. Colorado requires that the person making a will to dispose of real property be twenty-one years; those seventeen years of age may make a valid will bequeathing personal property. In Connecticut anyone eighteen years old may make a valid will of both real estate and personal property. In Delaware one must be twenty-one years of age or over. In the District of Columbia males over twenty-one and females over eighteen may make a will disposing of real estate and personal property. Those eighteen years of age may make a will disposing of both real estate and personal property in Florida. In Georgia the minimum age is fourteen years for disposing of both real estate and personal property. Those over twenty-one may will both real estate and personal property in Hawaii. In Idaho the minimum age is eighteen for both classes of property. Illinois requires that males be over twenty-one. females eighteen years or more to dispose of both real estate and personal property. In Indiana, Iowa, Kansas and Kentucky those twenty-one years or over may will real estate and personal property. Any person sixteen years or over in Louisiana may make a will disposing of real estate and personal property. In Maine the minimum age is twenty-one years, but any married woman or widow of any age may dispose of real estate and personal property by will. In Maryland the minimum age for men is twenty. one, for women eighteen, regarding both real estate and personal property. The minimum age in Massachusetts and Michigan is twenty-one years for disposal of both real estate and personal property. The minimum age in Minnesota is twenty-one years for men, eighteen years for women as to all classes of property. In Mississippi the minimum age is twenty-one for disposal of all property. In Missouri all persons twenty-one years of age and over may make a valid will of any kind of property; males over eighteen may bequeath personal property. In Montana those over eighteen may dispose of real estate and personal property. The minimum age in Nebraska is twenty-one years for all kinds of wills, though a married woman, irrespective of age, may make a valid will. In Nevada real estate and personal property may be disposed by those eighteen years and. over. New Hampshire requires that the person making a will be twenty-one years of age, or married. Any person over twenty-one years may will real estate and personal property in New Jersey and New Mexico. In New York the minimum age at which a person may will real estate is twenty-one; the minimum age for willing personal property is eighteen. In North Carolina the minimum age for real estate and personal property is twenty-one. In North Dakota the minimum age is eighteen for disposing of both real estate and personal property; in Ohio twenty-one for both real estate and personal property; in Oklahoma eighteen for disposal of real estate and personal property. Oregon permits men twenty-one years and over and women over eighteen years to will real estate and personal property. To dispose of any kind of property by will in Pennsylvania one must be over twenty-one years of age. In the Philippine Islands the minimum age for willing real estate and personal property is eighteen years. Puerto Rico bars all persons under fourteen years from making valid wills. In Rhode Island one must be twenty-one years to will real estate and personal property, and eighteen years to bequeath personal property. Anyone twenty-one years or over may will real estate and personal property in South Carolina; fourteen-year-old males and twelve-yeah old girls may will personal property. In South Dakota a person must be over eighteen years to dispose of real estate and personal property. In Tennessee a will of real estate may be made only by those twenty-one years or more; personal property, however, may be bequeathed by males fourteen years old and females over twelve years. One must be over twenty-one to dispose of real estate and personal property in Texas and Vermont. In Utah any person over eighteen may similarly dispose of property. Virginia requires that the person making a will of real and personal property be twenty-one years or over; those over eighteen years may bequeath their personal possessions. A person making a will of real estate and personal property in Washington must be twenty-one years of age in the case of men, eighteen years in the case of women. In West Virginia the law allows any person except infants to dispose of their property, whether real estate or personal. The rule in Wisconsin is that anyone over twenty-one, or any married woman over eighteen, may will real estate and personal property. In Wyoming anyone over twenty-one may dispose of all his property by will.

Question How many witnesses are required to execute a valid will?

Answer Two witnesses in Alabama, Alaska, Arizona, Arkansas, California, Colorado, Delaware, District of Columbia, Florida, Hawaii, Idaho, Illinois, Indiana, Iowa, Kansas, Kentucky, Maryland, Michigan, Minnesota, Mississippi, Missouri, Montana, Nebraska, Nevada, New Jersey, New Mexico, New York, North Carolina, North Dakota, Ohio, Oklahoma, Oregon, Pennsylvania, Rhode Island, South Dakota, Tennessee, Texas, Utah, Virginia, Washington, West Virginia, Wisconsin and Wyoming. Three witnesses are required in Connecticut, Georgia, Maine, Massachusetts, New Hampshire, South Carolina and Vermont.

Question What is a nuncupative will?

Answer This is an oral will made during the last illness of the deceased, in the presence of witnesses, respecting the disposition of his personal property after death. Soldiers in actual service and mariners at sea may verbally dispose of their wages and personal property to any amount, provided they are in actual fear or peril of death, or in expectation of immediate death from an injury received that day. Most states recognize some form of oral will. But as to this, see Question 22.

Question In which states are oral wills legal?

Answer Alabama—A verbal or oral will is valid only when personal property bequeathed does not exceed $500. Such a will must be made during the last illness of the deceased, at his dwelling or where he resided ten days or more, except when the testator is taken ill away from home and dies before his return. It must be shown that the deceased called upon persons present, or some of them, to bear witness that the statement is his will. Oral wills made by soldiers and sailors in actual service or mariners at sea are also valid in Alabama.

Alaska—An oral will is permitted if the deceased's words,

or substance thereof, are reduced to writing within thirty days after they are spoken and the writing probated after fourteen days and within six months after such words are spoken. Any mariner at sea or any soldier in military service may dispose verbally of his wages or other personal property.

Arizona—A verbal will is allowed if made in the last sickness of the deceased, where property does not exceed $50 in value. Three competent witnesses must testify that the testator called on some person to take notice and bear testimony that such is his will, and that the testimony, or its substance, was reduced to writing within six days after the making of such will. Where this is done, the amount that may be disposed of is without limit.

Arkansas—An oral will must be made at the time of the last illness of the deceased in the presence of at least two witnesses. The amount is limited to $500. Such a will must be proved not less than twenty days nor more than six months from the date thereof; it must be reduced to writing and signed by the witnesses within fifteen days after the will is made.

California—Amount limited to $1,000. An oral will must be proved by two witnesses present at the time it was made, one of whom was asked by the testator, at the time, to bear witness that such was his will. In addition, the deceased must have been, at the time, in actual military service in the held or doing duty while at sea. Finally, the deceased must have been in actual contemplation, fear or peril of death, or in expectation of immediate death from an injury received that same day. The verbal statement of the deceased must be reduced to writing within thirty days after the making.

Delaware—An oral will is-valid if confined to personal property not exceeding $200 in value. It must have been pronounced in the last illness of the deceased before two witnesses, be reduced to writing within three days, attested by the signatures of the witnesses, provided the testator dies before the expiration of the said three days or subsequently becomes incapable of making a will.

District of Columbia—An oral will is invalid, except in the case of soldiers and sailors in actual military service who may dispose of wages and personal property by word of mouth. Such as will must be proved by two witnesses and reduced to writing within ten days after its making.

Florida—It must be proved by three witnesses present at the time of making. The oral will must have been made during the deceased's last sickness and be reduced to writing within six days from making. Personal property only may be disposed of in this way.

Georgia—It must be made during the last illness of the deceased at the place where he resided for at least ten days preceding the declaration, except in case of sudden illness and death away from home. Three witnesses are necessary to prove such a will.

Idaho—It must be reduced to writing within thirty days after making. The will must be probated not less than fourteen days after the testator's death.

Illinois—An oral will is valid for transfer of personal property only, if reduced to writing within twenty days after the making, or within ten days after the deceased's death. It must be proved by at least two disinterested witnesses present at the time of its making.

Indiana—It must be made in the testator's last illness, be witnessed by at least two people and reduced to writing within fifteen days after the words are spoken. Valid only to extent of $100 worth of personal property.

Iowa—Personal property up to $300 may be disposed of by a verbal will if witnessed by two competent persons. Those in actual military or naval service may dispose of all their personal estate orally.

Kansas—To be valid, the verbal will must be reduced to writing and witnessed by two disinterested persons within ten days after words are spoken. It must be proved that the testator called upon some person or persons present when words were spoken who bore witness that the words were his last will.

Kentucky—Only a soldier in actual service or a mariner at sea may dispose of personal effects verbally, provided it is done ten days before death, in the presence of two competent witnesses and reduced to writing within sixty days after the words are spoken.

Louisiana—An oral will must be witnessed in the presence of a Notary Public by three persons residing in the place where the will is executed, or by five persons not residing in the place.

Maine—The oral will is allowed when made in the last illness of the testator, at his home or at the place where he resided ten days before making it. Maximum amount which may to disposed of in this way is $100. The will must be proved by three witnesses present at the time of making, who wen requested by the testator to bear witness that such was his will. If the words are not reduced to writing within six days after being spoken, they must be proved in court within 5 months. A soldier in actual service or a mariner at sea may verbally dispose of his personal estate.

Maryland— Verbal will is valid only as to soldiers in actual service or mariners at sea who may dispose of their wages, movables and personal property.

Massachusetts—Same rule as in Maryland.

Michigan—Maximum amount is $300. The will must be proved by two competent witnesses; this applies to soldiers in actual military service and mariners on shipboard.

Mississippi—It is valid only when made during the testator's last illness. The maximum amount is $100, unless it is proved by two witnesses that the testator called them to bear witness to his will. Such a will cannot be proved after six months unless reduced to writing within six days of speaking. There is a soldier and sailor provision.

Missouri—The maximum amount to be disposed may not exceed $200; it must be proved by two witnesses and that the testator, in his last sickness, at his home, called some person to witness the will. Proof of such will must be given within six months after words are spoken or substance of words reduced to writing within thirty days. Wills of soldiers and sailors are governed by the common law.

Montana—An oral will is valid when proved by two witnesses present at the making thereof, one of whom, at least, was asked by the testator to bear witness that such was his will. The maximum value is set at $1,000; the testator at the time must have been in actual military or marine service and the will must have been made in the expectation of immediate death from injury received that day; the will must be proved within six months and not less than fourteen days after the death of the testator.

Nebraska—The maximum amount is $150. The will must be proved by three witnesses present at the making and that the testator called them to witness his oral will; must be made during testator's last illness at home or while taken sick away from home. Unless reduced to writing within six days after oral declaration, will is not allowed. These rules are not applicable to soldiers in service and mariners on ships.

Nevada—The maximum value is $1,000; must be proved by two witnesses present at making thereof; must be made during last illness and proved not less than fourteen days nor more than three months after words are spoken.

New Hampshire—The maximum value is $100; must be declared in presence of three witnesses who were requested by testator to bear witness thereto, or be made during testator's last illness, at his usual dwelling place or away from same if taken ill while away from home and died before his return, or unless a memorandum of the oral will was reduced to writing within six days.

New Jersey—An oral will bequeathing personal property exceeding $80 is invalid unless it is proved by the oaths of at least three Witnesses present at the making thereof and unless the testator requested the persons present to bear witness to his verbal will or words to that effect; the will must be made during the testator's last illness, in his house or where he was a resident for ten days or more, except where the deceased was surprised or taken sick while away from his home and died before returning to his dwelling place.

New Mexico—An oral will is not valid except when made by a soldier in actual service or a mariner on shipboard.

New York—Only soldiers in service and mariners at sea may bequeath personal property by oral will; such a will must be made within the hearing of two persons and its execution proved by at least two witnesses.

North Carolina—min oral will must be proved by at least two witnesses present at time verbal will was made; the will must have been made during the testator's last sickness and, in his own residence, or where he had previously resided.

North Dakota—The maximum amount is $1,000; must be proved by two witnesses who were present at making; the deceased must have been in actual military service in the field or doing duty on shipboard at sea; in either case, he must be in fear or peril of immediate death from injury received the same day that the will was made.

Ohio—The oral will must be made in the last sickness of the testator; it must be reduced to writing and subscribed by two competent witnesses within ten days after the verbal declaration.

Oklahoma—The maximum amount is $1, 000; must be proved by two witnesses who were present at the making thereof, one of whom was asked by the testator at the time to act as a witness. In addition, the testator must have been in actual military service in the field or doing duty on shipboard at sea and must have been in actual contemplation, fear or peril of death, or in expectation of immediate death from an injury received that same day.

Oregon—Oral wills apply only to soldiers in service and sailors at sea.

Pennsylvania— An oral will is valid only if made during testator's last illness, in his own home or one in which he resided for at least ten days before making it, or where he is taken sick while away from home and dies before returning. If property bequeathed is over $109 in value, the oral will must be proved by two witnesses present at the time of the making thereof, and that the testator requested persons present to witness his will; words spoken must be reduced to writing within six days after they are spoken, but no proof of the words spoken can be received after six months from the speaking thereof unless they are reduced to writing.

South Carolina—An oral will disposing of personal property in excess of $501 is invalid unless proved by the oaths of three or more witnesses who were present when the will was made and requested by the testator to witness his will. The will must be made in the testator's last illness and in his house or plate where he died; proof of such will cannot be made after six months from the time the words were spoken unless reduced to writing within six days after the making of such will and then not after one year.

South Dakota—The maximum amount is $1,000; must be proved by two witnesses present at time words were spoken.

Tennessee—An oral will is unenforceable if over $250 in value, unless proved by two disinterested witnesses present at the time the words were spoken; witnesses must have been requested by the testator himself to bear witness thereto; the will must have been made in the testator's last illness in his own home or where he had previously resided at least ten days, except where he was taken sick while away from his home and died before returning.

Texas—An oral will is valid if made during the last illness of the deceased; must be made at his home, unless he was taken sick away from home and dies before returning; no oral will allowed when personal property bequeathed exceeds $30 in value unless proved by three credible witnesses; must be proved within fourteen days from testator's death and not after six months from the date of speaking, unless committed to writing within six days therefrom.

Utah—Where the estate is not in excess of $1,000, an oral will may be admitted to probate at any time after deceased has been dead ten days and within six months after the words are spoken; words must be reduced to writing within thirty days after they are spoken.

Vermont—An oral will may not pass personal possessions exceeding $200 in value; memorandum in writing must be made by a person present at the time of the making of said will within six days from making of the oral will.

Virginia—Only soldiers in military service and mariners at sea may dispose of personal property by oral will.

Washington—An oral will is allowed if personal estate does not exceed $200; it must he made during testator's last illness and must be proved by two witnesses who were requested by the testator to witness his will; must he reduced to writing.

West Virginia—Only soldiers and sailors in actual service may dispose of personal property by verbal will.

Wisconsin—A verbal will disposing of an estate in excess of $150 in value is of no effect unless proved by the oath of three witnesses present when the will was made who were requested-by the testator to witness it; it must be made during the last illness of testator in his home or dwelling or where he resided for ten days prior to the making of the will, except when he was taken sick while absent from his home and died before returning.

Question   While on maneuvers, a soldier is fatally stricken with a heart attack. A few minutes before he dies, he orally tells the commanding officer that he wants his buddy, John, to have his diamond ring. Is this a valid will?

Answer   Yes. Verbal wills of soldiers in actual service and sailors at sea are generally valid. In many states. Such wills are recognized as legal without any specified number of witnesses.

Question   What is a holographic will?

Answer   A holographic will is one written entirely by the hand of the testator; It may be written in pencil or ink, or partly in both. It may take the form of a letter or a notation or a note It must be entirely written, signed and dated by the testator Not all states recognize such wills, nor are witnesses required in all jurisdictions allowing holographic wills but as to this see the following question.

Question   Which jurisdictions are holographic wills recognized as legal?

Answer   Alaska: no witnesses.

Arizona: no witnesses.

Arkansas: three disinterested witnesses

California. no witnesses.

Connecticut: three witnesses.

Idaho: no witnesses.

Kentucky: no witnesses.

Louisiana: no witnesses.

Montana: no witnesses.

Mississippi: no witnesses.

Nevada: no witnesses.

New York: Holographic wills by soldiers or sailors while in

actual military service, or by a mariner while at sea, are valid during the war. Such wills are unenforceable and invalid upon the expiration of one year following discharge from military service, provided testator still retains capacity to execute a valid will. Where, after his discharge from service, a testator still lacks such capacity, the holographic will is valid and enforceable until the expiration of one year from the time capacity is regained.

North Carolina: Must appear that the will was found among the valuable papers of the testator. Testator's handwriting must be proved by three witnesses.

North Dakota: no witnesses.

Oklahoma: no witnesses.

Puerto Rico: no witnesses.

South Dakota: no witnesses.

Tennessee: substantially the same provisions are in force as in North Carolina.

Texas: no witnesses.

Utah: no witnesses.

Virginia: no witnesses.

West Virginia: no witnesses.

Question   John writes a letter to a sister in which, after referring to land and his intention to build thereon, he tells her: "If I die, or get killed in Texas, the place must belong to you and would not want you sell it." Is this a good will?

Answer   Yes. This is a holographic will and is valid in these states in which such wills are legal.

Question   After the testator's death, a letter is found which reads as follows: "Many accidents may occur to me which might deprive my sisters of that protection which it would be my duty to afford; and in that event, I must beg that you will attend to putting them in possession of two-thirds of what

I may be worth, appropriating one-third to Mrs. Jones and her child, in any manner that may appear most proper." Is this a good will?

Answer Yes. A will may take the form of a letter if signed and properly witnessed.

Question After John's death, a paper is found which reads as follows: "This is good to Miss Ruby Cox for $600, as payment for care and attendance rendered by her to me in my last sickness; this $600 is to be collected out of my estate, providing, however, I die a bachelor." Can Ruby collect the $600?

Answer Yes. This is a good will, since it is conditioned on John's dying a bachelor and was not to take effect until after his death.

Question To be valid, must a will be signed by the testator?

Answer Yes. It must be signed either by the testator or by some person in his presences and at his express, direction and request.

Question Is a will otherwise good if signed by a cross or mark?

Answer Yes. What constitutes a sufficient signature largely depends on the custom of the time and place, the habit of the individual and the circumstances of each particular case.

Question A testator begins to sign his name, writes the syllable "Rob," then desists because of physical weakness. Would failure to complete his name make the entire will void?

Answer Yes. The testator must write all that he intended to write in order that there may be a sufficient signing. In the above case, for example, it could be argued that the reason the testator did not complete his signature is that he changed his mind after writing "Rob."

Question A will, written wholly in the handwriting of the testator, begins, "I, John Doe, declare this to be my last will." The testator's name appears nowhere else in the will. The will is enclosed in a sealed envelope on which is written, in the testator's handwriting,' "My will. John Doe." Is this a valid will?

Answer No. Because it is not signed by the testator.

Question What is meant by attestation?

Answer To attest a will means to witness it at the request of the testator, the party making it, and to sign one name to it as a witness.

Question	An attorney who has drawn a will proposes to the testator that the lawyer and his stenographer witness it. Calling her from an adjoining room into his office, the lawyer and his stenographer both sign the will in the testator's presence and without objection from him. Is this a valid will?
Answer	Yes. The general rule is that the testator must request the witnesses to attest the will. This request may be made either expressly by the testator or by another in his behalf, or may be inferred from his conduct and from all the facts and circumstances attending the witnessing. When the testator allowed the lawyer and his stenographer to witness the will, he gave his consent to their attestation.
Question	May one who is to be a beneficiary under a will be a witness to it?
Answer	No. It is generally provided by statute that a bequest to at subscribing witness shall be void but that the will shall be otherwise valid.
Question	Is it necessary that witnesses see the testator sign the will?
Answer	No, in the absence of a statutory requirement. However, it is frequently provided by statute that the testator shall either sign the will in the presence of witnesses, or shall acknowledge his signature before them. Any words, acts or conduct of the testator which, reasonably interpreted, amount to a recognition of the signature as his, in the presence of witnesses who are aware of such words, acts or conduct, is a sufficient acknowledgment.
Question	A will is so folded that the testator's signature is invisible to the witnesses who, nevertheless, sign the document. Is this a sufficient acknowledgment of the testator's signature?
Answer	No. The witnesses must see the testator's signature.
Question	Is it necessary that witnesses sign at the end of the will?
Answer	No, not unless a statute specifically provides for it. The attestation need not be in any particular place, provided there is us evidence that the witnesses, in signing their names, have the intention of attesting the document. To avoid any question, however, it is wise to have witnesses sign at the end of the will.
Question	Is it necessary that witnesses to a will sign it in the presence of the testator?
Answer	Generally, yes. This requirement is met when the witnesses

sign in such a way that the testator can see the act of attestation.

Question   While a testatrix is in one room, her will is signed by witnesses in an adjoining room. The testatrix can observe the signing pi the will it she looks. Is this sufficient?

Answer   Yes. Provided the witnesses are so situated that the testatrix can see them when they sign, it is immaterial where the witnesses are.

Question   Tom is tone deaf. He executes his will in the olhce of his lawyer who draws it in accordance with his instructions. The attorney brings in two secretaries to act as witnesses. After Tom reads the will and signs it, the attorney shows him a pad on which he writes: "Is this your will and do you wish Miss Smith and Miss Jones to witness it for you?" Tom nods his head, whereupon the lawyer hands the will to the secretaries who attest it, signing their names as witnesses. The secretaries see Tom nod but neither see what is written on the pad. Is the will properly executed?

Answer   Yes. Unless the statute expressly requires it, witnesses need not know the nature of the instrument they are signing; in this case, it is sufficient that they know they are witnessing some instrument which Tom has signed and means to acknowledge as his own.

Question   An ailing testator signs his will, but before the witnesses can affix their signatures, he falls into a state of unconsciousness. The witnesses sign, nevertheless. Is such a will valid?

Answer   No. The witnesses must sign in the testator's presence while he is conscious.

Question   What is meant by the capacity to make a will?

Answer   What constitutes capacity to make a valid will is defined by the laws of the various states; by such laws all persons except infants and those of unsound mind have the capacity to execute a valid will.

Question   A person makes a will while suffering severely from cancer. The will is later sought to be upset on the ground that the testator lacked the capacity to make a valid will. Would the court, in the absence of other proof, permit the will to be upset?

Answer   No. Capacity to make a will may exist, even though the testator be old, weak and ill, even to the point of death, at the time he executes the will, as long as his mind functions normally.

Question A testator suffers from an incurable disease which his physician ceases to treat because he can do nothing to arrest its progress. On the day he signs his will, he lies helpless in his bed, unable to carry on conversation or to understand questions put to him. Does this indicate capacity to make a will?

Answer No. Here, obviously, the testator is unable to comprehend the significance of his act in signing the will. If proved, this fact will probably suffice to upset the document.

Question In his will, a testator directs that part of his intestines shall be made into violin strings and the rest of his body wvitrified into lenses, explaining that he has an aversion to funeral pomp and Wishes his body to be made useful to mankind. Are these eccentric instructions sufficient to upset a will on the ground that the testator lacks mental capacity?

Answer No. Mere eccentricity, although proper to be considered as hearing thereon, does not of itself amount to insanity.

Question A testator who is chronically insane makes a will during a lucid interval. Is such a will valid?

Answer Yes, although the existence of a lucid interval will be exceedingly difficult to prove. If, however, such a lucid interval could be proved, the will might be sustained.

Question What constitutes "undue influence" in the writing of wills?

Answer The exercise of such influence over the testator as to control his mental operations, inducing him to dispose of his property in a way which he would not have done had he been left free to act according to his own wishes. Undue influence deprives the person making a will of his free agency, and if such influence is proved, the instrument will be upset. Mere advice, argument or persuasion, however, which do not deprive the testator of his mental freedom, are not considered undue influence.

Question What is the effect of a will obtained by undue influence?

Answer Such a will is void to the extent that it is the result of such influence.

Question Due to the constant and repeated urgings of his wife, a testator who is ill makes a will leaving all his property to his wife, ignoring completely his children by a former marriage. Is such a will valid?

Answer Probably not. It is true that the will was made voluntarily, but it was made clearly for the sake of the respite or peace of mind gained. Very likely such a will could be upset on the ground that it was obtained by undue influence.

Question   A son urges his mother to make a will in his behalf which she later does. Is such a will considered to be obtained by undue influence?

Answer   No. A son has a right to urge his mother to make a will in his behalf, and if the only effect of such promptings is to arouse her affections or to appeal to her sense of duty, they are unobjectionable.

Question   A bedridden testator is led to make a certain will in consequence of a threat by his wife that she will leave him if he refuses to do so. Is such a will considered to be obtained by undue influence?

Answer   Yes.

Question   An aged and feeble testator makes a will. disinheriting a faithful son at the demand of his wife with whom the son has quarreled. Is such a will valid?

Answer   No. In this case, the wife would be considered legally as having exercised undue influence over her husband.

Question   May a blind or deaf person make a valid will?

Answer   Yes. Proof however must be given that the contents were made known to the testator.

Question   Tom, a habitual drunkard, executes a will, properly witnessed, leaving his property to his wife and children. is such a will good?

Answer   Yes. Intoxication does not of itself invalidate one's will. Courts incline to sustain a drunkard's will when it is just and natural and the circumstances of execution favorable.

Question   A testator executes one will, then afterwards executes a second one. He later writes a third will, declaring that the first one shall be his last will if he dies before a given date; otherwise the second one is to be his last will. Is such a will (or wills) valid?

Answer   Yes. Wills may be written so as to take effect in the alternative with reference to a stated contingency or happening of an event.

Question   In his will, a testator leaves a legacy of $1,000 to John, forgetting to add John's last name. is such a legacy good?

Answer   Yes. Omissions may be supplied where the context of the will indicates a name or thing has been inadvertently left out. Where both names of a legatee or devisee are omitted in the will, oral evidence as to their identity may not be introduced to supply the missing blanks. In this case, evidence is admissible to establish the identity of John's last name.

Question A will is read over to a testator who intends that a legacy shall be given to a certain person. This individual's name is unintentionally omitted in the will, the omission being we observed by the testator. May the unnamed beneficiary claim a share under the will?

Answer Where the contents of the will are actually communicated to the testator, the will takes effect as written and no evidence can be received to add to or subtract therefrom. Hence, the unnamed beneficiary has no claim.

Question May you cut off your spouse completely in a will?

Answer No. In most states. As a rule, you must leave your spouse. by will, at least the same part of the estate which she (or he) would have received if there had been no will. In many states, she may refuse to accept what you provide for her in your will, taking advantage of her statutory rights instead, unless you give her all the law requires.

Question A testator, on slight but insufficient proof, clings to the belief that his wife is unchaste and one of his daughters illegitimate. In his will, he completely disinherits that daughter. Can the will be upset?

Answer No. An ill-founded belief, not actually amounting to insanity, does not destroy capacity to make a will. Where one indulges in an aversion, however harsh, which is the conclusion of a reasoning mind, on evidence, no matter how slight or inaccurate, one's will cannot on that account be overturned or upset.

Question What happens to the bequests in your will where there isn't enough money in the net estate to pay them all?

Answer All the bequests are reduced proportionately, unless you have made specific provision that some are to be preferred over others.

Question A will provides that, after payment of the testator's debts, all the debts of his mother are to be paid out of "my estate." Is such a clause binding on the testator's heirs?

Answer No. Only the testator's debts need be paid.

Question A testator leaves John a valuable diamond ring. John, however, dies before the testator, leaving two children. May John's children claim the diamond ring after the testator's death?

Answer   No. John's heirs get nothing, the property passing either under the residuary clause (a clause which passes the testator's estate left after payment of debts, costs of administration and specific bequests), or will be distributed as intestate property—that is, as if no will had been made and in accordance with the laws of the testator's state.

Question   What is meant by probating a will?

Answer   To probate a will means to prove before some officer or tribunal, authorized by law, that the document offered is the last will and testament of the deceased person whose act it is alleged to be; that it has been executed, attested and published as required by law, and that the testator was of sound and disposing mind. In short, when a 'will is probated its validity is established. Until a will is duly probated or proved, courts will not recognize any powers of the one named in the will as executor, nor any one claiming under the will, such as a devisee or legatee. Where probate is refused, it is presumed that the deceased died intestate (without a will).

Question   Two beneficiaries under a will enter into an agreement whereby one of them agrees that he will not contest its probate Is such an agreement binding?

Answer   Yes, if made with full knowledge of all the facts and risks involved.

Question   How may a will be revoked?

Answer   A will may be revoked or cancelled at the pleasure of the testator. Ordinarily, it is revoked by mutilation, by a subsequent writing revoking the will, or by certain changes in the circumstances and conditions of the testator, from which a revocation will be implied by law.

Question   May a written will be revoked orally?

Answer   No.

Question   A testator throws his will into a fire, intending to destroy it. The will, slightly singed, is snatched from the flames by another person. Is the will still valid?

Answer   No. Any visible burning of the will, not matter how slight, if caused with the intent to revoke, is sufficient to constitute a revocation. Mutilation, which is one of the recognized methods of revoking a will, includes any impairment of the material upon which the will is written, such as tearing, burning, etc.

Question	A testator makes an unsuccessful attempt to burn his will. He dies a few minutes later. Has his will been revoked?
Answer	No. Unsuccessful attempts to burn a will effect no revocation; neither does a burning of the envelope containing the will, providing the latter remains untouched.
Question	John brings a will to a blind testator at the latter's request. The testator, after feeling the seals of the envelope in which the will is enclosed, requests John to throw it into the fire. John, pretending to do so, substitutes another paper for the will, calling the testator's attention to the odor and the crackling of the burning paper. The testator dies in the belief that his will has been revoked. Has it?
Answer	No. The revocation must be in a manner prescribed by law, not verbally.
Question	A testator tears up his will under the mistaken impression that he has not properly executed it. He orders a new and similar writing to be made out but dies before executing it. May the torn instrument be introduced as the will?
Answer	Yes. It is admissible on the ground that an intent to revoke was lacking, since the testator destroyed the will while laboring under a misapprehension.
Question	A testator executes a will in duplicate; keeping one copy for himself and depositing the other with his bank. Shortly afterward, the testator destroys his copy of the will and dies before he can request the bank to destroy the copy it holds. Has the testator revoked the will?
Answer	Yes. If a will is executed in duplicate a mutilation by the testator of that part in his own custody constitutes a revocation of both copies. The law presumes that the mutilation of the one duplicate was done with the intent to revoke bot copies
Question	A testator, while sane, makes a valid will. He becomes insane and destroys the will. Is his will still good?
Answer	Yes. As much mental capacity is required to revoke a will as to make one. The testator's insanity deprived him of the necessary intent to revoke.
Question	A testator executes two wills. Wishing to revoke one of them, he destroys the wrong document by mistake. Does his act revoke the paper he intended as his will?
Answer	No. There is no mutilation of the will, since the testator did not intend to revoke it, having torn it up erroneously.
Question	Does a mutilation of a will, induced by undue influence

constitute a revocation?

Answer No, since the testator is not acting of his own volition but under the influence of another.

Question A testator cancels his signature and those of the subscribing witnesses, accompanying the act with this memorandum: "In consequence of the death of my wife it becomes necessary to make another will. " He dies before such will is made. Is his first will revoked?

Answer Yes. The revocation of the will is absolute and complete, the testator clearly indicating such intention by cancelling the signatures and leaving a memorandum to that effect.

Question In his will, a testator leaves his house to a brother. A few weeks before the testator's death, he sells the house to a third party. Can the brother still claim the house?

Answer No. When the testator sold the house the will was revoked was far, at least, as the house was concerned.

Question You make a will prior to your marriage. A few years after the marriage, a child is born. Is your will, executed before the marriage, valid?

Answer No. Marriage followed by the birth of a child, absolutely revokes the will and your wife and child will inherit your property in the manner prescribed by law in cases of intestacy—i.e., where no will is left—
rather than in accordance with your personal wishes.

Question You make a will after your marriage, but in it you mention nothing about children. A few years later, a child is born. Will your child inherit upon your death?

Answer Yes. In most states the birth of a child does not work the entire revocation of a prior will; it does so only to the extent of the interest which the child would have taken had there been no will. A wise precaution is to make a new will, or codicil, upon the birth of each child.

Question A few years after his marriage, a testator adopts a child. Is his will revoked to the same extent as if the child were born in wedlock?

Answer Yes, in many states. When an adopted child is given the status of one born in wedlock, his adoption has been held to revoke a prior will as effectually as would natural children of the marriage.

Question What is the effect of the birth of illegitimate children upon a prior will?

Answer It depends wholly upon the statute of each particular state.

As a rule, if not recognized or in some way made legitimate under the statute, the birth of an illegitimate child after a will is executed has no effect and the illegitimate child will not inherit.

Question   A testator makes a will leaving all his property to his wife. A few years later, he secures a divorce. Before he can make a new will he dies. Does the divorce revoke the will so as to prevent the ex-spouse from inheriting?

Answer   No. Revocation of a previously executed will is not implied by law from the fact that the testator obtains a divorce. But where the divorce is accompanied by a property settlement, it is sometimes held that the change of circumstances is sufficient to cause an implied revocation of a prior will.